THE PERFECT COVER LETTER

THIRD EDITION

RICHARD H. BEATTY

WILEY

JOHN WILEY & SONS, INC.

To those who struggle with the chore
of effective letter writing and are
looking for professional guidance and help.

For general information on our other products and services please contact our Customer
Care Department within the United States at (800) 762-2974, outside the United States at
(317) 572-3993 or fax (317) 572-4002.

Wiley also publishes its books in a variety of electronic formats. Some content that appears
in print may not be available in electronic books. For more information about Wiley
products, visit our web site at www.wiley.com.

Library of Congress Cataloging-in-Publication Data:

Beatty, Richard H., 1939–
    The perfect cover letter / Richard H. Beatty.—3rd ed.
        p.   cm.
    Includes index.
    ISBN 0-471-47374-X (pbk. : alk. paper)
    1. Resumes (Employment).   2. Cover letters.   I. Title.
HF5383.B325   2003
650.14′2—dc21

                                        2003053483

Printed in the United States of America.

10   9   8   7   6   5   4   3   2   1

PREFACE

Welcome to the *Third Edition* of the best-selling *The Perfect Cover Letter*! This edition has been updated and expanded to include the latest thinking and trends in cover-letter writing, providing you with a complete arsenal of cover letters that will serve you well throughout your job-hunting campaign. I am confident you will find it a great reference guide that will help you write excellent letters that both impress employers and enhance the probability of landing interviews and job offers.

Curiously, most job seekers invest considerable time and effort in preparing the ultimate resume; however, few invest nearly the same effort and care needed to prepare the employment cover letter—the very first document that meets the eyes of the employer when receiving a resume. As a seasoned employment professional, I have always found this a curious phenomenon, especially since it is the cover letter that serves as the initial introduction to prospective employers.

Much has been written about the importance of first impressions when it comes to the job interview. We have been led to believe that the initial impression created by the employment candidate, during the first few minutes of the interview, will have significant impact on the outcome. If this impression is positive, the chances of employment are greatly enhanced. Conversely, a negative first impression is bound to result in an unfavorable outcome.

But what about the cover letter? Isn't it true that, as the first contact with the employer, this document is bound to have a major impact (good or bad) on that employer's initial impression of your candidacy? Absolutely!

The cover letter can have a very significant impact on the outcome of the employment application process. If well written, it can create excitement and interest in your employment candidacy, compelling the employer to invite you for an interview. On the other hand, if poorly written, it can prove immediately fatal to an otherwise well-orchestrated job-hunting campaign. In fact, one survey of over 500 employment professionals shows that a full 76 percent of employers will immediately eliminate candidates whose cover letters are poorly written and contain typos or grammatical errors.

Beyond the importance of first impressions, the cover letter also provides the employment professional with the opportunity to gauge a number of other important competencies that are not so apparent from the resume document alone. These are factors that can easily affect the decision to screen you either in or out of further hiring consideration, for example:

1. Written communication skills.
2. Organization skills.
3. Impression of overall intelligence.
4. Sense of focus and priorities.
5. Personal style.
6. Social skills.
7. Business/management philosophy.
8. Operating style.
9. Management style.
10. Technical knowledge.

Undoubtedly, the overall design, content, and construction of the re-sume cover letter can play a major role in the overall effectiveness of your job search. With so much riding on it, it is important, therefore, to commit the necessary time and effort to this too-often-ignored, but critical, element of your job-search program.

The purpose of this book is to provide you with a practical, hands-on manual for design and construction of highly effective cover letters that enhance and support your job-search objectives. Its emphasis is on practical application. Material is presented in a logical, step-by-step manner, supported by concrete examples, thereby facilitating the letter-writing process.

We begin by discussing the purpose and importance of cover letters and contrasts good and poor cover-letter design. We proceed through the advance preparation steps essential to put the right information at your fingertips. A chapter is included that gives practical advice con-cerning the kinds of information that should be included in the cover letter and that which is best left out. This is followed by many chapters providing detailed instructions for writing a variety of cover letters for different situations. Each provides many real-life examples for easy reference.

New to this edition are three chapters that fully round out your job-search, letter-writing arsenal. These include Chapter 10 (Networking Cover Letters), Chapter 11 (The Resume Letter), and Chapter 12 (Em-ployment Thank You Letters). Each type of letter plays a critical role in enhancing the success of your job-hunting program and needs to be part of your employment repertoire.

By following the advice in this book and by using the sample letters provided as models, you will be well equipped to write interesting and dynamic letters that significantly improve the success of your job-hunting campaign.

Happy letter writing and my best wishes to you for a highly success-ful employment campaign!

RICHARD H. BEATTY

West Chester, Pennsylvania

CONTENTS

1

AN INTRODUCTION TO COVER LETTERS

The cover letter that accompanies your employment resume is perhaps one of the most important letters you will ever write. Other than your resume, it is the single key document that will introduce you to a prospective employer and, if well-written, pave the way to that all important job interview. It is an integral part of your overall job-hunting campaign, and it can make or break you, depending upon how well it is written. Construction of this document should, therefore, be given very careful attention. The care that you give to writing this letter will certainly be a major factor in getting your job search off to an excellent start. Conversely, a poorly written letter is sure to scuttle your campaign before it even begins.

The Purpose of the Cover Letter

Before you can expect to write an effective cover letter, you must understand its purpose. Without a clear understanding of what this letter is intended to accomplish, chances are it will be poorly designed, vague, and generally ineffective. On the other hand, understanding the purpose of this letter is paramount to maximizing its impact and effectiveness.

What is the purpose of the cover letter? What is it intended to do?

Well, first and foremost, it is a business letter used to transmit your resume to a prospective employer. So, it is a business transmittal letter. Second, it is a letter of introduction. It is used not only to transmit your resume but also to introduce you and your background to the employer. Third, and importantly, it is a sales letter, intended to convince the prospective employer that you have something valuable to contribute and that it will be worth the employer's time to grant you an interview.

To summarize, then, the purpose of a cover letter is:

1. To serve as a business transmittal letter for your resume.
2. To introduce you and your employment credentials to the employer.
3. To generate employer interest in interviewing you.

Certainly, knowing that these are the three main objectives of a well-written cover letter will provide you with some basic starting points. We will be further discussing these objectives and the related elements of good design throughout this book. For now, it is important to simply keep these objectives in mind as we further explore the topic of constructing effective cover letters.

From the Employer's Perspective

When contemplating good cover letter design and construction, it is important to keep one very important fact in mind: The cover letter must be written from the employer's perspective.

Stated differently, good cover letter writing must take into consideration the end result you seek in employer action. More specifically, you want the employer to grant you an interview, so it is important to understand those factors that will motivate an employer to do so. To understand this important phenomenon, it is necessary to realistically address the following questions:

1. How does the employer read the cover letter?
2. What are the key factors the employer is looking for (and expects to find) in the cover letter?
3. What are the motivational factors that will pique the employer's curiosity and create a desire to interview you?

I think you will agree that these are some important questions to ask if you are to be successful in designing cover letters that will be truly helpful to your job-hunting program. You must pay close attention to the needs of the prospective employer, rather than just your own, if you expect to write cover letters that will motivate him or her to take action. Cover letters must, therefore, be "employer focused" rather than "job-searcher focused" if you want to really maximize their overall effectiveness.

Top sales producers have always known that the most important principle in sales success, whether selling goods or services, is selling to the needs of the buyer. What is the customer really buying? Where are the priorities? What specific needs does he or she need to satisfy? Without knowing the answers to these questions, it is easy for the salesperson to emphasize product characteristics and attributes that have absolutely no relationship to the customer's real needs, and deemphasize characteristics and attributes that are truly important. The result—no sale!

Ideally, therefore, it is important to research your target companies very well to determine what it is that they are buying (i.e., looking for in a successful employment candidate). If you are conducting a general broadcast campaign covering several hundred companies, such individual company research may simply not be feasible. If, on the other hand, you are targeting a dozen or so employers for whom you would really like to work, such research is not only feasible but should be considered an "absolute must." Careful advance research, in this case, will pay huge dividends, returning your initial investment of time and effort manyfold.

Even in the case of the general broadcast campaign, where you have targeted several hundred companies, there are some things that you can do to focus your cover letters on the real needs of these employers. Here are some guidelines for conducting meaningful employer needs research:

1. Divide your target list of employers into industry groupings.

2. Using industry trade publications and key newspapers (available in most libraries), thoroughly research each industry grouping for answers to the following questions:

    a. What is the general state of this industry?

    b. What are the major problems faced by companies in this industry?

    c. What are the barriers or roadblocks that stand in the way of solving these problems?

    d. What knowledge, skills, and capabilities are needed to address these problems and roadblocks?

    e. What major trends and changes are being undertaken by companies in this industry?

    f. What new knowledge, skills, and capabilities are needed to successfully orchestrate these changes and trends?

Having conducted this type of general research, you are now in a position to better focus your cover letter on key needs and areas of interest to the majority of companies in each of your targeted industry groupings. This provides you with the opportunity to showcase your overall knowledge, skills, and capabilities in relation to those important needs areas. Such focusing substantially increases your chances for hitting the employer's bull's-eye, which will result in job interviews.

Where you can narrow your list to a dozen or so key companies, individual company research can have even greater payoff. Here, you have the opportunity to really zero in on the specific needs of the employer, and you can bring into play a number of research techniques for doing so. The research you do here can, in fact, be tailored to each individual firm; so you can substantially increase your probability of success and up, by quite a bit, the number of potential interview opportunities.

In many ways, the methodology used in conducting single-firm research is similar to that already described for industry-wide research. You will note some of these similarities as you review the following guidelines for researching the single firm.

1. Determine the firms you would like to target for individual research (firms for which you would really like to work).

2. Using industry trade publications and key newspapers (available at your local library) as well as annual reports, 10K forms, and product literature (available from the target firm's public affairs and marketing departments), thoroughly research for answers to the following questions:

    a. What is the general state of the company?

    b. How does it stack up against competition?

    c. What are the key problems and issues with which it is currently wrestling?

    d. What are the key barriers that must be removed in order to resolve these problems/issues?

    e. What knowledge, skills, and capabilities are needed to remove these key barriers?

    f. What are the company's strategic goals?

    g. What are the key changes that will need to come about for realization of these goals?

    h. What new knowledge, skills, and capabilities will be needed to bring about these critical changes?

Here, as with research of industry groupings, individual company research enables you to use the cover letter to highlight your knowledge, skills, and capabilities in areas that are of importance to the firm. In the case of individual firm research, however, there is the added advantage of being able to tailor the cover letter to target your qualifications to very specific, known needs of the employer. This can provide you with a substantial competitive advantage!

Another technique that you should employ when doing individual firm research is networking. If you don't already belong, you might consider joining specific industry or professional associations to which employees of your individual target firms belong. Using your common membership in these organizations as the basis, you can call these employees for certain inside information. Here are some questions you might consider asking:

1. Is the firm hiring people in your functional specialty?
2. Are there openings in this group now?
3. Who within the company is the key line manager (i.e., outside human resources) responsible for hiring for this group?
4. What are the key things this manager tends to look for in a successful candidate (e.g., technical knowledge, skills, style)?
5. What key problems/issues is the group currently wrestling with?
6. What kinds of skills and capabilities are they looking for to address these issues?
7. What are the major strategic changes this group is attempting to bring about?
8. What qualifications and attributes is the group seeking to help them orchestrate these strategic changes?

Answers to these questions can give you a tremendous competitive advantage when designing an effective cover letter and employment resume. You will have substantial ammunition for targeting and highlighting those qualifications of greatest interest to the employer. Here, you can make the most of your opportunity for successful self-marketing by focusing on the critical needs not only of the organization but of the functional hiring group as well. Clearly, this is a technique you should employ if you want to maximize your chances of getting hired!

The underlying principle behind this needs research methodology, whether industry grouping or individual company research, is that organizations are always looking for individuals who will be "value adding"—that is, individuals who can help them solve key problems and realize their strategic goals. These are the candidates who are seen as the value-adding change agents—the leaders who will help move the company ahead and enhance its competitive position rather than allow it to stagnate. Employer needs research will allow you to design effective cover letters that can truly set you apart from the competition and substantially improve your chances for landing interviews.

How Cover Letters Are Read

Although, in many cases, such practice can be self-defeating, the great majority of resumes and accompanying cover letters are often sent to the attention of the employment or human resources department. It is here that the cover letter probably least serves the interests of the job seeker.

The truth of the matter is that most human resources and employment professionals are unlikely to pay much real attention to the cover letter. In the course of a year, it is estimated that the employment manager of a medium- to large-size company may read over 20,000 resumes along with accompanying cover letters. This considerable experience has led most professionals to conclude that cover letters seldom add little meaningful information to that already provided in the resume itself. Such letters are usually of the "broadcast" variety and are frequently redundant to the resume.

Having learned this, the employment or human resources manager will normally give the cover letter only a cursory glance and first concentrate on reading the resume. This is because the resume details the specifics of the candidate's background and qualifications and is used for comparing these qualifications with the hiring manager's specific requirements.

When reading the cover letter, the employment manager will usually look to see if it is the mass-mailed "broadcast" kind, or if it is more personal or specific to the company. Managers usually try to ferret out letters that indicate any kind of firsthand association with the company—for example, friends of employees and executives, shareholders, and local community leaders. These letters normally require a more personal response, and care is taken so that an inappropriate form response is not accidentally sent. Unfortunately, however, cover letters of a less personal nature normally receive very little initial attention from employment/personnel professionals.

If this is the case, then why write a book on cover letters? Why take time to provide advice to people on how to best design and construct such letters if they are barely read? The answer to this is fairly simple. I am recommending that, in most cases, you not send your cover letter and resume to the human resources or employment departments of the firms that you have targeted for your mailing. Instead, I am strongly recommending, where at all possible, that you address your correspondence to a specific individual within the corporation. This person should be at a fairly high level and should be within the particular business function or discipline most closely related to the position for which you are applying. Thus, if you are a tax accountant, you will want to direct your letter to the director of taxes. Similarly, if you are an engineering manager, you will want to write to either the director or vice president of engineering. If you are already at the director or vice president level, however, you should correspond with the firm's president or chief executive officer.

What is the logic behind my recommendation to send your cover letter and resume directly to the line function rather than the personnel department? Again, the answer is fairly simple. The reason is that the employment manager, in many cases, has knowledge only of those positions that are currently open. He or she may be totally unaware of the future hiring needs of line managers—needs that they are thinking about filling at some future point. In some cases, "some future point" can be as immediate as next week or next month. A well-written cover letter accompanying a resume may be just the thing that causes the hiring executive to move ahead and fill the position now.

A line manager will usually read the cover letter a little more thoroughly than will the employment manager. The motivation is different. The employment manager is simply looking for credentials that match a current open position, whereas the line manager (the one who does the actual hiring) is looking for solutions to existing problems; new ideas for bringing improvement to the organization; understanding of new, emerging business concepts and trends; and so forth. In general, this manager is looking for ways to add value to the organization. He or she will thus tend to read the cover letter and resume more closely, with a view toward addressing the aforementioned need categories. Your well-constructed cover letter and resume may suggest that you can help to address these needs—that you are someone who could add real value to the organization. The result could well be an invitation for an employment interview.

Here is further evidence that supports the importance of target company needs research. If, through good research, you can pinpoint the specific problems, trends, and strategic objectives of this employer (and specifically the hiring manager), you have a much better basis for constructing a highly focused cover letter that addresses them. If your particular knowledge and qualifications suggest that you may have some good answers, and you have highlighted this in your cover letter, you have created what is known in economics as the "accelerator effect" and have increased the probability of an employment interview manyfold.

In summary, the way a cover letter is written should directly relate to the way it will likely be read. Where possible, through good advance research (either by industry grouping or by individual firm), it should be designed to highlight your qualifications to solve contemporary problems, facilitate current trends, apply state-of-the-art methodology, and drive desired strategic change. To maximize effectiveness, your letter must convey a sense that you are a person who will be adding value in those key areas where the target company is looking for answers and desires improvement.

Your cover letters thus need to be "reader aligned" rather than "writer aligned." They must address the real needs of the prospective employer, not just your needs. The key to such alignment is advance research, without which your letters will be like buckshot in a strong wind rather than a well-aimed single shot directed at the center of the bull's eye. It is likely to miss the target and cripple an otherwise well-planned job search process.

The Advantages of a Good Cover Letter

This chapter has, I hope, served to increase your awareness of the importance of a good cover letter to your job-hunting campaign. Let's explore this topic in greater depth, however, so that you can more fully appreciate its importance.

It is important to realize, right from the beginning, that the employment cover letter is, in most cases, the very first contact that you will have with the employer. The important thing to realize here is that if the letter is poorly written, many employers may never even bother to go as far as to read your resume; it can be an automatic turnoff, leading the employer to move on to the next cover letter and resume. A poor cover letter can screen you out of the employment selection process before you even get started. You may never have an opportunity to compete.

The appearance of the cover letter, as with the resume, makes a personal statement about you to the prospective employer. If it is ill-conceived, disorganized, and sloppy, it will suggest that you are disorganized and sloppy in your work. It may also suggest that you don't care about the impression you make on others and that you are not particularly well motivated. Likewise, if the cover letter rambles and lacks focus, it may suggest that you are verbose and nonfocused, generally lacking a sense of organization.

By contrast, a well-planned, well-written, highly focused cover letter will make quite a different statement about you to a prospective employer. It will suggest that you are very thorough and careful, and that you take a great deal of pride in your work. It may also suggest that you are well-organized, strategic, focused, and results-oriented. Thus, there is a decided upgrade to your job-hunting campaign through the use of well-planned, well-designed cover letters that create a highly favorable impression.

Besides a favorable image, a good cover letter also provides you with an excellent vehicle to highlight key aspects of your credentials that are closely related to major needs of the prospective employer. In this sense, if well-written and properly focused, it can do a much better job of selling your value to a prospective employer than can the accompanying resume, which leaves the employer with the challenge of wandering through a maze of information to ferret out those qualifications that are truly relevant to his or her contemporary needs. The cover letter can thus become an extremely forceful sales tool for persuading the employer that a job interview would be a very worthwhile investment.

It cannot be overemphasized that the effectiveness of the cover letter as a sales tool is directly related to the quality of your advance research on the real needs of the firms on your target list. Although well-organized and well-written, if your cover letter fails to focus on the major needs of the employer, a substantial opportunity to maximize its sales effectiveness is lost, and the direct result will likely be dramatically reduced interview opportunities.

It's up to you, then, to make the cover letter what it can be—a significant enhancement to your job-hunting campaign or a negative drain that casts you in a poor light and substantially detracts from your access to excellent job and career opportunities. The choice is yours!

The following chapters will provide you with the help you will need to plan, construct, and write cover letters that are targeted to the needs of employers and that maximize your opportunities for employment interviews—the perfect cover letter, so to speak.

2

COVER LETTER FORMAT

Writing a successful cover letter will require that you use a proper business letter format—one that is widely used and accepted for this purpose. It is, therefore, important that you familiarize yourself with those letter formats that are most commonly used and recognized as acceptable for cover letters.

By "format," I mean the actual design and physical layout of the letter. This is different from the "content" of the letter, which means the topics and matter discussed in the text. This chapter will deal with the subject of proper letter format. The subject of content (what should be included in or excluded from the cover letter) will be dealt with in considerable depth in the ensuing chapters of this book.

The Importance of Format

The physical layout and design of a cover letter is important to its effectiveness for several reasons.

First, good layout and design enhance appearance and serve to create a favorable impression on the part of the reader. A letter that is well-designed, properly spaced, and neat will create a positive image of you as an individual. It will suggest to prospective employers that you are logical, neat, and well-organized. Conversely, an improperly or poorly designed letter can convey just the opposite and thus leave a negative impression.

Second, a neat, concise, and well-organized format will substantially improve readability, thereby enhancing communications and increasing the probability that your cover letter will be read. Additionally, a good format will properly highlight the important aspects of your credentials, thus improving the chances of successfully marketing yourself to prospective employers.

Third, failure to employ an acceptable business letter format may suggest that you are ignorant of common business practices or, that you simply don't consider conventional business practices important. Neither impression will help your cause and may, in fact, detract substantially from your self-marketing efforts and your overall job-hunting plan.

It should be evident from this discussion that using an acceptable cover letter format is important to your job search. Therefore, you should be sufficiently motivated to follow the conventional advice offered in this chapter.

Acceptable Letter Format

A random sampling of numerous cover letters received by our human resources consulting firm suggests that there are three acceptable formats commonly used by job seekers in the preparation of their employment cover letters. These three letter formats and their respective percents of usage, as determined by this survey, are shown below:

Type of Cover Letter Format	Percent Used
Full Block	49%
Block	34
Modified Block	17

In reviewing the results of this survey, it is important to note that virtually 100 percent of the cover letters received by our consulting firm utilized only three formats. And since the only basic difference between the block and the modified block format is that the latter utilizes paragraph indentation, there are actually only two basic letter formats acceptable for the employment cover letter. These are the full block and the block/modified block versions.

If the overwhelming practice among job seekers is to use one of these two designs, common sense indicates that these formats must have something going for them, and that departure from them is likely to result in an aberration that might jeopardize your cover letter's effectiveness.

Some would argue that in cover letter preparation, as in resume preparation, you should "dare to be different." The usual argument here is that the unconventional format stands out from the pack and thus compels reading. Those of you who might be somewhat swayed by this logic are encouraged to think more broadly about the issue.

The assumption is that the unconventional design not only compels attention but also suggests to prospective employers that you are a creative and resourceful individual who will contribute new ideas and fresh thinking to the organization. Are you convinced? Although the logic is impeccable, the reality of the end result can spell a job-hunting disaster of the first order. You've heard the saying that one man's junk is another man's treasure? How about the saying that beauty is in the eye of the beholder? The point here is that there are differences in human perception. Actually, what you feel is a clever, creative approach that sets you apart from the hordes may, in the eyes of the prospective employer, automatically classify you as a nonconforming, maladjusted, nonconventional person, ignorant of acceptable business practice, immature, foolish, rebellious, or something else less than complimentary.

When it comes to designing your cover letter, my best advice is to leave creativity to the artists and stick with proven, time-tested approaches that will effectively promote your employment credentials and thus enhance your prospects of landing an interview. I have read thousands of cover letters and resumes, and I can assure you that your interests will be much better served by sticking with common business practice. I have seen many attempts at cleverness, creativity, or humor fall far short of the author's intended mark and substantially detract from an otherwise effective employment presentation. Why take the chance?

We will use the rest of this chapter to thoroughly familiarize you with the two most common cover letter formats—the full block and the block/modified block. Each of these will be described in detail and illustrated by examples. First, however, it will be necessary to discuss the standard components of the business letter so that their nomenclature will be clearly understood.

Components of the Cover Letter

The standard components of a cover letter, in the order in which they are positioned in the actual letter, are: return address, date, address, salutation, body, complimentary closing, signature, typist identification, and enclosure line. Although seldom used, some additional, optional components are: attention line, subject line, copy line, and postscript. Let's examine each of these components for correct positioning, usage, content, and punctuation. Proper use of these components is paramount to correct cover letter design and format.

Return Address

The return address is the address to which you wish return correspondence directed. In the case of the employment cover letter, this is normally the address of your residence. In certain cases, it could be the address of your current employer, if your employer is aware of your job search. Use of a business address is generally discouraged, however, since this can create some doubt concerning the reasons for such openness; for example, are you being involuntarily terminated for poor performance?

The following are examples of return addresses:

125 East Warrington Street
West Chester, PA 19382

Apartment #325
Windham Gate Apartments
Post Road at Surrey Place
Waterford Leas, MA 25118

P.O. Box 235
Burlington, VT 87246

Close examination and comparison of these examples will reveal some common characteristics, as follows:

1. The first letter or numeral of each line is directly aligned with the first letter or numeral of the preceding line. No lines are indented.
2. The first line is the specific location: number and street address, apartment number, post office box number, etc.
3. Each succeeding line moves from a more specific to a more general location (e.g., Apartment #325, to Post Road at Surrey Place, to Waterford Leas, MA).
4. The final line of the return address contains the name of the town or city, state, and postal zip code.
5. Each word of the address starts with a capital letter.
6. The name of the town or city is followed by a comma.
7. The name of the state is abbreviated, using the Postal Service abbreviation, and is followed by the appropriate Postal zip code.

The positioning of the return address on the page, determined by the type of letter format chosen (full block or block/modified block), is discussed later in this chapter. Depending upon the length of the letter, however, the first line of the return address is normally positioned between 6 to 10 lines from the top of the page. Additionally, all lines comprising the return address are single-spaced.

Date

The date shown on the cover letter is the actual date on which the letter is written. This date is positioned on the very next line below the return address and is aligned so that the first letter or numeral of the date is directly in line with the first letter of the return address line that precedes it.

The date is usually displayed in a month–day–year sequence. The first letter of the month is always capitalized, and the name of the month is spelled out in full—never abbreviated. Thus, the following is an example of a correct date:

March 3, 1998

The day of the month is always followed by a comma.

Although not as commonly used in the cover letter, a day–month–year sequence is also acceptable business practice. Thus, the following example would be considered acceptable practice:

3 March 1998

In this case, the order of the dateline is day, month (the first letter of which is capitalized), and year. There is no punctuation used in this format.

Although acceptable business practice, the day–month–year date sequence is normally used for business-to-business correspondence. It is also commonly used in military and other government correspondence. Generally, this form of correspondence is considered to be more formal than is recommended for the cover letter, which is actually a more personal type of correspondence (i.e., individual writing to organization rather than organization writing to organization). For this reason, I much prefer and recommend the month–day–year sequence—the format commonly associated with personal correspondence. In my judgment, it allows you to come across as personal and sincere rather than formal or stuffy. In most cases, I believe, this approach will tend to foster closer personal feeling on the part of the reader and thereby better serve your interests.

Address

The address is the address of the organization to which you are sending your cover letter. This component comprises the addressee's name and title, the name of the addressee's organization, and the organization's full mailing address.

In both the full block and block/modified block formats, as will be illustrated later in this chapter, the address section is blocked flush with the left margin of the letter. It is also single-spaced, with the first line starting on the next line following the date.

The first line of the address begins with the name of the individual to whom you are writing. Always use his or her formal name, including middle initial, if known.

Whenever a business letter is addressed to a specific individual, as should always be the case with a good cover letter, the addressee's name should be preceded by a courtesy title (Mr., Ms., Mrs., Dr., etc.). Although no longer an absolute requirement in general business correspondence, the use of the courtesy or social title adds a personal touch to the correspondence, which is lost when only the addressee's name is used. It also connotes a measure of respect for the person as one who will make certain judgments on behalf of their organization concerning your employment candidacy.

A word of caution here, however! The special sensitivities created by the strong desire of most women to be accepted as equals of men in the business world suggest that, in most cases, you should not attempt to distinguish a woman's marital status. As with the use of the social title "Mr.," which has come to designate either a married or unmarried man, the social title "Ms." has come to represent a married or unmarried woman. When addressing a woman in the employment cover letter, therefore, it is recommended that the courtesy title "Ms." be used.

There is only one exception to the use of "Ms." in cover letters addressed to women. In cases where you are personally acquainted with the addressee and you know that she prefers to be addressed as either "Mrs." or "Miss," it is acceptable to use these titles. If you are in doubt concerning this preference, however, I strongly advise using "Ms."

In the case of attorneys and medical doctors, the social title does not precede the addressee's name. Instead, the appropriate title follows the name, as below:

Mary D. Smith, M.D.
John R. Smith, Esq.

Curiously, it has not become practice to use "Esq." when addressing women attorneys. This has to do with the derivation of the word

"Esquire," which was historically used by the British as a term of respect for a man (not necessarily a lawyer). Hence, the title of Esquire is never used with a female attorney.

Although in most modern business letters, use of a company or business title is considered optional, it is recommended that such titles be used in the employment cover letter. There are several reasons for this. First, such titles are courteous and convey respect for the person to whom you are writing. Second, the title used (Vice President of Engineering, Director of Manufacturing, etc.) frequently designates the department or function in which you are interested and may thus ensure that your letter gets to the right place in the event of a recent change in personnel. Finally, the title may well serve to jog your memory, at some future point in your job search campaign, if you are trying to remember whether you have written to a specific department within one of your target companies.

The length of the business title will determine whether or not it should be included on the same line as the addressee's name. If it is relatively short, it is fairly common practice to include it on the same line. It is also considered quite acceptable to include the title as a separate line immediately below the name, particularly when the title is a lengthy one. The key here is aesthetics.

Should inclusion of the title on the first line create a noticeable imbalance, move it to the second line (directly beneath the addressee's name). Unless the title is unusually long, it is not considered acceptable practice to split it between two lines. Although not normally recommended, it is advisable in such unusual cases to use some abbreviations in an effort to accommodate the title on a single line.

On the line immediately following the company title, you may want to include the department or function in which the person is employed, unless this function or department is already included in the person's job title. If no such functional or departmental designation is included in the addressee's job title, and you are certain of the exact name, you will probably want to include it as part of the address section of the cover letter. The operative word here is "exact." If you are not sure of the exact name of the department or function, either call the company for verification or leave it out of the address entirely.

In the case where job title is included on the first line of the address along with the addressee's name, the name and title are separated by a comma. In all cases, the first letters of both the job title and department or function are capitalized.

The next line of the address section should show the formal name of the organization. You may elect to use either the company's full formal name or its official abbreviation—for example, either IBM Corporation or International Business Machines Corporation. Although it is generally acceptable to use such abbreviations as "Co.," "Corp.," or "Inc.," follow the company's own practice in this regard. Consult a reputable business directory or the firm's own stationery, if available, for correct spelling and abbreviations.

The street address immediately follows the name of the organization. It normally includes street number, directional quadrant (north, south, east, or west) where appropriate, and street name or title. Street numbers are normally spelled out up to ten; over ten they are represented by numerals. "Street" and "avenue" are not customarily abbreviated; however, "boulevard" is often abbreviated as "Blvd." The first letters of all words in the street address line are capitalized.

If a post office box is used instead of a street address, the common way of writing it is "P.O. Box _____." As with the street address, all initial letters are capitalized.

The final line of the address section of the cover letter contains the name of the town or city, the name of the state, and the zip code. The name of the town or city begins with a capital letter and is followed by a comma. The name of the state is abbreviated using the official abbreviation designated by the Postal Service. This is followed by the zip code.

Examples of typical address sections follow:

> Mr. William P. Denting, President
> The Keller Group
> 25 North Billings Road
> Northfield, MI 66258
>
> Ms. Sandra M. Lindstrom
> Director of Manufacturing
> S.D. Warren Company
> 118 Enterprise Way
> Chicago, IL 28395
>
> Michael F. Davingport, M.D.
> Crossworth Medical Institute, Inc.
> P.O. Box 345
> Kansas City, MO 19472

Ms. Katherine R. Lorring, Vice President
Public Affairs Department
Smith, Barnam and Jergeson, Inc.
4215 Worchester Blvd.
Portsmouth, NH 81375

Mr. David Bracksbee, Esq.
President
Bracksbee, Feathersom and Binker, Inc.
Nine Olympic Place
Seattle, WA 99836

Salutation

The salutation is used to greet the person to whom you are writing. In business letters, if the person to whom you are writing is not personally known, the common practice is to use "Dear," followed by the courtesy or social title (Mr., Ms., Dr., etc.) and then the person's surname. For example:

Dear Ms. Wilson:

Dear Dr. Arlingar:

Dear Senator Bacon:

Use of the first name or a nickname in business correspondence, although a growing trend, is not considered appropriate unless you have been personally introduced. Even then, it is important to carefully consider the closeness of the relationship before following this practice in your cover letter. Unless you are already on a first-name basis, it is best not to. This is especially true if the individual to whom you are writing is at a significantly higher level in the organization than you. Use of the first name in such a case could be considered discourteous or inappropriate and could prove fatal to your employment effort.

On the other hand, if you have been introduced on a first-name basis to the addressee, by all means use his or her first name in your correspondence. If this was only a chance meeting, you may need to recall the introduction in the opening paragraph, and the letter will usually need to be written in a more personal tone than that used in the typical broadcast cover letter. The basic principle is that the more personal the tone of your letter, the greater the probability of a personal response. A subtle reminder of personal connections with the reader will, in almost all cases, substantially improve your chances of an interview and possible employment. Use these personal connections, but don't abuse them.

Although this should rarely happen if you have been thorough in your research, sometimes you may need to address your cover letter to an organizational title or function, without having a specific name. Should you be unable to avoid this particular circumstance, then the salutation will need to be changed accordingly.

Since you will not know the gender of the person to whom you are writing, you will be unable to use the traditional salutation. In such cases, you may wish to use one of the following:

Dear Sir or Madam:

Ladies and Gentlemen:

Dear Sir:

Today, the greeting "Dear Sir" may appear somewhat sexist. For this reason, either of the other two choices is preferred.

In both the full block and block/modified block cover letter formats, the salutation is always placed flush with the left margin and positioned two to four lines below the last line of the address section.

Body

The body of the cover letter is positioned two lines below the salutation. It contains your message for the addressee. The exact positioning of this message will vary with the type of letter format chosen.

In the full block and block formats, all text, including the first line of each new paragraph, is positioned flush with the left margin. In the modified block format, however, the first line of each new paragraph is indented five spaces from the left margin.

The text of both medium-length and long letters is single-spaced, with double-spacing used to separate paragraphs. Although short quotations should be contained in the normal flow of text and separated by quotation marks, lengthy quotations (usually those exceeding 50 words) are completely set off from the text, in a single-spaced block with double spacing above and below the block. These longer quotations are also normally indented five spaces from both margins.

When the cover letter contains lists or enumerations, these are formatted similarly to lengthy quotations. Normally, such lists are treated as a block of text and separated from the regular text by double-spacing above and below. As with the long quotation, the items contained in the list are indented five spaces from both margins. List items that occupy more than one line of text are single-spaced, with double-spacing separating each complete item.

We will not attempt to cover the content of the cover letter body at this point, since it is the subject of a good portion of this book and will vary depending upon the kind of cover letter written.

Complimentary Closing

The complimentary closing is the word grouping used to bring the message or text to a close. It is positioned immediately following the body of the letter and just preceding the author's signature. The exact position depends upon the letter format chosen and is explained fully later in this chapter. Normal spacing between the last line of body text and the complimentary closing, however, is usually two spaces.

The complimentary closing you choose should bear some relationship to your familiarity with the reader. "Yours," "Best regards," "Regards," "Best wishes," and so forth, are considered somewhat informal and personal and are therefore normally reserved for persons with whom you have a fairly close relationship. "Sincerely," "Sincerely yours," and "Most sincerely," are friendly but a little less personal and are thus considered more appropriate for use with persons who are either unknown or unfamiliar to you.

A survey of several hundred cover letters received by our consulting firm revealed the following breakdown of usage of various types of complimentary closings:

Complimentary Closing	Percent Usage
Sincerely,	64%
Sincerely yours,	20
Very truly yours,	14
Yours very truly,	2

It should be pointed out that these were cover letters addressed to various members of our staff, to whom the writers were either unknown or unfamiliar. This seems to suggest that, where you are unfamiliar with the addressee, it is safe to use any of the first three complimentary closings shown on the preceding chart. If you are on fairly personal terms with the addressee, however, it is recommended that you use a more appropriate closing, such as "Yours," "Regards," "Best regards," "Best wishes," and so forth. Such closings are more in keeping with a friendly relationship.

You will note that the complimentary closing is always followed by a comma. You will also note that it is only the initial word whose first letter is capitalized. The rest are all in lower case.

Signature Line

The signature line is always positioned flush with the complimentary closing and at least four lines below it. This allows sufficient space for the author's signature. The exact positioning on the page depends upon the format of cover letter chosen, and is further explained later in the chapter.

The signature line contains the full formal name of the writer, including first name, middle initial (followed by a period), and surname. Although this may first appear overly formal in some cases, it should be remembered that the actual signature of the writer can be used to soften the tone of the signature line. Thus, if the author's formal name is Thomas J. Sanders, he might simply sign the letter "Tom" if that is in keeping with the nature of his relationship to the addressee.

Where the addressee is either unknown or unfamiliar to the author, it is recommended that the author sign his or her full formal name. Simply the first name or a nickname in such cases is considered inappropriate to the nature of the relationship.

Typist Identification

The initials of the person typing the letter are always shown flush with the left margin, two lines below the signature block. These initials are typed in lower case. Thus, if the typist's name is George B. Smith, the letters "gbs" would appear on the left margin.

In those cases where you have dictated the cover letter, but your secretary or administrative assistant has typed and signed it, the identification line would consist of your initials (in capital letters), followed by a colon and then the initials of the typist (in lower case). If your name is Samuel B. Higgins and your secretary's name is Linda D. Britting, the identification line would read "SBH:ldb."

Enclosure Line

Since your cover letter will normally include a resume as a separate enclosure, this fact should be noted in the enclosure line, which is positioned flush with the typist identification and two lines immediately below.

If there is only a single enclosure, such as your resume, the word "Enclosure" will suffice. If there are multiple documents enclosed (five, for example), this can be designated by "Enclosures (5)" or simply "Enclosures."

Letter Formats

As stated earlier in this chapter, there are, essentially, only two acceptable formats to be used with the cover letter. These are the full block and the block/modified block. Since the modified block represents only a very slight alteration of the block format, for purposes of our discussion, I will treat these two formats as one.

Let's now examine these formats.

The Full Block Format

The full block format is represented in Figure 2.1. As mentioned earlier, it is fairly popular and, according to my survey, it was used in 49 percent of several hundred cover letters received by our human resources consulting firm.

Figure 2.1 reveals the distinguishing characteristics of the full block format when contrasted with the block/modified block style. Note that all components of the full block format—the return address, date, address, salutation, complimentary closing, signature line, typist identification, and enclosure line—are completely flush with the left margin of the letter.

From a typing efficiency standpoint, this format is slightly preferred over the block/modified block style. Since all lines of the full block layout are flush with the left margin, there are no indentations, which saves key strokes and therefore cuts down on the time and cost of producing the letter. This is an important (but not overriding) consideration.

Another benefit of the full block format is its neat, crisp, and easy-to-read appearance. It looks very uniform, structured, formal, and

FIGURE 2.1   *Full Block Format*

XXXXXXXXXXXXXXX   (return address)
XXXXXXXXXXXXXXX
XXXXXXXXXXXXXXX   (date)

XXXXXXXXXXXXXXX   (address)
XXXXXXXXXXXXXXX
XXXXXXXXXXXXXXX
XXXXXXXXXXXXXXX
XXXXXXXXXXXXXXX

XXXXXXXXXXXXXXX   (salutation)

XXXXXXXXXXXXXXXXXXXXXXXXXXXXXXXXXXXXXXXXXXXXXXXXXXXXXXXXX
XXXXXXXXXXXXXXXXXXXXXXXXXXXXXXXXXXXXXXXXXXXXXXXXXXXXXXXXX
XXXXXXXXXXXXXXXXXXXXXXXXXXXXXXXXXXXXXXXXXXXXXXXXXXXXXXXXX
XXXXXXXXXXXXXXXXXXXXXXXXXXXXXXXXXXXXXXXXXXXXXXXXXXXXXXXXX

XXXXXXXXXXXXXXXXXXXXXXXXXXXXXXXXXXXXXXXXXXXXXXXXXXXXXXXXX
XXXXXXXXXXXXXXXXXXXXXXXXXXXXXXXXXXXXXXXXXXXXXXXXXXXXXXXXX
XXXXXXXXXXXXXXXXXXXXXXXXXXXXXXXXXXXXXXXXXXXXXXXXXXXXXXXXX
XXXXXXXXXXXXXXXXXXXXXXXXXXXXXXXXXXXXXXXXXXXXXXXXXXXXXXXXX
XXXXXXXXXXXXXXXXXXXXXXXXXXXXXXXXXXXXXXXXXXXXXXXXXXXXXXXXX

XXXXXXXXXXXXXXXXXXXXXXXXXXXXXXXXXXXXXXXXXXXXXXXXXXXXXXXXX
XXXXXXXXXXXXXXXXXXXXXXXXXXXXXXXXXXXXXXXXXXXXXXXXXXXXXXXXX
XXXXXXXXXXXXXXXXXXXXXXXXXXXXXXXXXXXXXXXXXXXXXXXXXXXXXXXXX

XXXXXXXXXXXXXXXXXXXXXXXXXXXXXXXXXXXXXXXXXXXXXXXXXXXXXXXXX
XXXXXXXXXXXXXXXXXXXXXXXXXXXXXXXXXXXXXXXXXXXXXXXXXXXXXXXXX
XXXXXXXXXXXXXXXXXXXXXXXXXXXXXXXXXXXXXXXXXXXXXXXXXXXXXXXXX
XXXXXXXXXXXXXXXXXXXXXXXXXXXXXXXXXXXXXXXXXXXXXXXXXXXXXXXXX

XXXXXXXXXXXXXXX   (complimentary closing)

XXXXXXXXXXXXXXX   (signature line)

XXX   (typist identification)

XXXXXXXXX   (enclosure line)

businesslike. It suggests to the reader that the author is likewise a neat, organized, structured, and businesslike person.

Although the full block format will likely serve you very well in your job-hunting campaign (and I would not hesitate to recommend its use), in my judgment, there may be some advantages to using the block/modified block format, instead. Let's take a look at these advantages.

Block and Modified Block Formats

As stated earlier in the chapter, the block and modified block letter formats are also very popular. In fact, according to my survey, these styles, when combined, account for an estimated 51 percent of all cover letters. This suggests that they are slightly more popular than the full block format.

Review of the block and modified block formats (see Figures 2.2 and 2.3) reveals that they are substantially similar. Both indent the return address and datelines so that the longest line of these components is flush with the right margin of the letter. The complimentary closing and signature lines are also indented. These latter two lines may be indented in one of the following ways:

1. Flush with the right margin.
2. Five spaces to the right of the center of the page.
3. Centered on the page.

Regardless of positioning, however, the first letters of both the complimentary closing and the signature line are in vertical alignment.

The only difference between the block and the modified block is that the modified block provides for indentation of paragraphs. The first line of each new paragraph is indented five spaces. In the block layout, the first line of each paragraph is positioned flush with the left margin.

The remaining components in these two formats (address, salutation, body, typist identification, and enclosure line) are positioned flush with the left margin and are essentially identical to the full block format.

Like the full block format, the block and modified block formats are neat, well-organized, and easily read. In my judgment, however, they have two clear advantages over the full block format.

FIGURE 2.2   *Block Format*

                                         (return address)   XXXXXXXXXXXXXXX
                                                             XXXXXXXXXXXXXXX
                                             (date)   XXXXXXXXXXXXXXX

XXXXXXXXXXXXXXX   (address)
XXXXXXXXXXXXXXX
XXXXXXXXXXXXXXX
XXXXXXXXXXXXXXX
XXXXXXXXXXXXXXX

XXXXXXXXXXXXXXX   (salutation)

XXXXXXXXXXXXXXXXXXXXXXXXXXXXXXXXXXXXXXXXXXXXXXXXXXXXXXXXXXXXXXXXX
XXXXXXXXXXXXXXXXXXXXXXXXXXXXXXXXXXXXXXXXXXXXXXXXXXXXXXXXXXXXXXXXX
XXXXXXXXXXXXXXXXXXXXXXXXXXXXXXXXXXXXXXXXXXXXXXXXXXXXXXXXXXXXXXXXX
XXXXXXXXXXXXXXXXXXXXXXXXXXXXXXXXXXXXXXXXXXXXXXXXXXXXXXXXXXXXXXXXX

XXXXXXXXXXXXXXXXXXXXXXXXXXXXXXXXXXXXXXXXXXXXXXXXXXXXXXXXXXXXXXXXX
XXXXXXXXXXXXXXXXXXXXXXXXXXXXXXXXXXXXXXXXXXXXXXXXXXXXXXXXXXXXXXXXX
XXXXXXXXXXXXXXXXXXXXXXXXXXXXXXXXXXXXXXXXXXXXXXXXXXXXXXXXXXXXXXXXX
XXXXXXXXXXXXXXXXXXXXXXXXXXXXXXXXXXXXXXXXXXXXXXXXXXXXXXXXXXXXXXXXX
XXXXXXXXXXXXXXXXXXXXXXXXXXXXXXXXXXXXXXXXXXXXXXXXXXXXXXXXXXXXXXXXX

XXXXXXXXXXXXXXXXXXXXXXXXXXXXXXXXXXXXXXXXXXXXXXXXXXXXXXXXXXXXXXXXX
XXXXXXXXXXXXXXXXXXXXXXXXXXXXXXXXXXXXXXXXXXXXXXXXXXXXXXXXXXXXXXXXX
XXXXXXXXXXXXXXXXXXXXXXXXXXXXXXXXXXXXXXXXXXXXXXXXXXXXXXXXXXXXXXXXX

XXXXXXXXXXXXXXXXXXXXXXXXXXXXXXXXXXXXXXXXXXXXXXXXXXXXXXXXXXXXXXXXX
XXXXXXXXXXXXXXXXXXXXXXXXXXXXXXXXXXXXXXXXXXXXXXXXXXXXXXXXXXXXXXXXX
XXXXXXXXXXXXXXXXXXXXXXXXXXXXXXXXXXXXXXXXXXXXXXXXXXXXXXXXXXXXXXXXX
XXXXXXXXXXXXXXXXXXXXXXXXXXXXXXXXXXXXXXXXXXXXXXXXXXXXXXXXXXXXXXXXX

                              (complimentary closing)   XXXXXXXXXXXXXXX

                                        (signature line)   XXXXXXXXXXXXXXX

XXX   (typist identification)

XXXXXXXX   (enclosure line)

FIGURE 2.3   *Modified Block Format*

                                (return address)   XXXXXXXXXXXXXXX
                                                    XXXXXXXXXXXXXXX
                                      (date)   XXXXXXXXXXXXXXX

XXXXXXXXXXXXXXX   (address)
XXXXXXXXXXXXXXX
XXXXXXXXXXXXXXX
XXXXXXXXXXXXXXX
XXXXXXXXXXXXXXX

XXXXXXXXXXXXXXX   (salutation)

    XXXXXXXXXXXXXXXXXXXXXXXXXXXXXXXXXXXXXXXXXXXXXXXXXXXXXXXX
XXXXXXXXXXXXXXXXXXXXXXXXXXXXXXXXXXXXXXXXXXXXXXXXXXXXXXXXXXXX
XXXXXXXXXXXXXXXXXXXXXXXXXXXXXXXXXXXXXXXXXXXXXXXXXXXXXXXXXXXX
XXXXXXXXXXXXXXXXXXXXXXXXXXXXXXXXXXXXXXXXXXXXXXXXXXXXXXXXXXXX

    XXXXXXXXXXXXXXXXXXXXXXXXXXXXXXXXXXXXXXXXXXXXXXXXXXXXXXXX
XXXXXXXXXXXXXXXXXXXXXXXXXXXXXXXXXXXXXXXXXXXXXXXXXXXXXXXXXXXX
XXXXXXXXXXXXXXXXXXXXXXXXXXXXXXXXXXXXXXXXXXXXXXXXXXXXXXXXXXXX
XXXXXXXXXXXXXXXXXXXXXXXXXXXXXXXXXXXXXXXXXXXXXXXXXXXXXXXXXXXX
XXXXXXXXXXXXXXXXXXXXXXXXXXXXXXXXXXXXXXXXXXXXXXXXXXXXXXXXXXXX

    XXXXXXXXXXXXXXXXXXXXXXXXXXXXXXXXXXXXXXXXXXXXXXXXXXXXXXXX
XXXXXXXXXXXXXXXXXXXXXXXXXXXXXXXXXXXXXXXXXXXXXXXXXXXXXXXXXXXX
XXXXXXXXXXXXXXXXXXXXXXXXXXXXXXXXXXXXXXXXXXXXXXXXXXXXXXXXXXXX

    XXXXXXXXXXXXXXXXXXXXXXXXXXXXXXXXXXXXXXXXXXXXXXXXXXXXXXXX
XXXXXXXXXXXXXXXXXXXXXXXXXXXXXXXXXXXXXXXXXXXXXXXXXXXXXXXXXXXX
XXXXXXXXXXXXXXXXXXXXXXXXXXXXXXXXXXXXXXXXXXXXXXXXXXXXXXXXXXXX
XXXXXXXXXXXXXXXXXXXXXXXXXXXXXXXXXXXXXXXXXXXXXXXXXXXXXXXXXXXX

                    (complimentary closing)   XXXXXXXXXXXXXXX

                          (signature line)   XXXXXXXXXXXXXXX

XXX   (typist identification)

XXXXXXXX   (enclosure line)

First, they provide more space for text than does the full block, because of the positioning of the return address and date line in relation to the first line of the address. You will note in the block and the modified block that the first line of the address is on the very next line following the date. By contrast, the full block requires three spaces between the dateline and the first line of the address. Either the block or the modified block layout will thus save three lines and allow more text in the body of the letter.

The second advantage these two formats have over the full block design is their tone. The full block is a structured, businesslike layout, which suggests a more formal, impersonal tone. This is the tone that you might expect when writing business to business.

By contrast, however, the other formats resemble that most widely used in personal correspondence. More specifically, the indentation used in both the block and modified block designs is similar to that in a personal letter and suggests a less formal, more personal tone that is more in keeping with the tone you hope to create with the cover letter.

Although either the block or modified block style is perfectly acceptable for the cover letter, if given the choice, my selection would be the block format for the following reasons.

The cover letter is neither "business-to-business" nor "person-to-person" (personal) correspondence. Instead, it is "person-to-business." Thus, the format chosen should most closely match this "in-between" relationship.

As stated earlier, the full block format is the most formal, suggestive of business-to-business correspondence. On the other hand, the modified block format is identical to that used in most personal correspondence and may be slightly too personal in tone. By contrast, the block format (with its blocked paragraphs and indented return address, date, complimentary closing, and signature lines) is a cross between the full block and the modified block formats. Therefore, it seems most appropriate to the nature of the relationship and the "person-to-business" tone that the cover letter should convey.

In keeping with this logic, if you are well acquainted with the person to whom you are writing, by all means use the modified block format. In this case, both the full block and the block layouts are less appropriate, and the modified block format will better serve your purpose.

Enough said about the subject of cover letter format. Now let's move on to the actual cover letter itself. What should go into the body of the letter? What are the important points that need to be covered? How do you write an interesting cover letter that effectively markets your qualifications and motivates an employer to set up a job interview? These are the important subjects that will be answered in the ensuing chapters.

The next two chapters will deal with the important differences between good (effective) and poor (ineffective) cover letters. In each case, the elements and characteristics of good and poor cover letters are fully explained. To further make the point, actual samples of both are provided for your review and close examination.

3

CHARACTERISTICS OF GOOD COVER LETTERS

In this chapter, we will be discussing good cover letters and their characteristics. What makes one cover letter effective and another drab and ineffective? Perhaps the best way to meaningfully address this question is to discuss the elements and characteristics of good and bad cover letters, and show some examples, so that you can actually see the differences. The focus of this chapter will be on good cover letters; the focus of the next chapter will be on those that are poorly written and ineffective.

Before getting started with our discussion, I strongly encourage you to spend a few moments carefully reviewing the four examples of good cover letters at the end of this chapter. You will find this review particularly helpful in understanding the points I will be making.

Important Elements

Close examination of the sample cover letters provided at the end of this chapter will reveal that they exhibit the following similarities:

1. An introductory paragraph that:
   a. Is "interest generating."
   b. States or implies employment interest.
2. A "value-selling" paragraph that:
   a. Demonstrates your ability to be value adding.
   b. Highlights your key strengths and abilities.
3. A "background summary" paragraph that briefly summarizes your relevant education and experience.
4. A statement that either "compels or ensures follow-up action."
5. A "statement of appreciation."

We will now proceed with a detailed discussion of each of these key elements for a fuller understanding of their importance to the success of an effective cover letter.

Introductory Paragraph

The introductory paragraph is extremely key to the effectiveness of the employment cover letter. Essentially, it has two important objectives.

The first is to grab the reader's attention and thus compel the reader to continue reading the letter. The second is to establish your interest in employment (the purpose of the letter).

The first paragraph can render the cover letter useless if it fails to compel sufficient interest on the part of the reader to warrant his or her further reading. It is important, therefore, to get the reader's attention right from the start by opening your letter in an interesting manner.

Usually, if the reader senses that yours is one of those "mass-mailed, broadcast variety" letters that has been sent to hundreds of other executives, there is little incentive to read it. On the other hand, if there is some indication of personal knowledge of or connection with the company and the letter seems tailored to that specific reader or his or her organization, the reader's interest is usually heightened immediately and the probability of readership increases greatly.

Generally, there are three effective techniques for creating a personal, customized touch in the introductory paragraph. These are:

1. Use of personal contact.
2. Use of specific company knowledge.
3. Use of a compliment.

Each of these can be reasonably effective in adding just that right amount of personal touch. Let's examine some examples of these three techniques.

Of the three interest-generating techniques mentioned here, the most effective is the use of personal contact. Cover letter sample C at the end of this chapter provides a good illustration of effective use of this technique.

You will note in sample C that the author has mentioned the name of a company employee, Walt Stevenson, in the very first sentence of the introductory paragraph. Although the author does not state this, the implication is that Stevenson and he are personal friends or acquaintances. Because of the wording, there is no way for the letter's recipient, Craig Deters, to know just how close this relationship is. Stevenson could be a very close personal friend or simply a brief acquaintance.

In this situation, where there is no immediate way to confirm the nature of the relationship, the general tendency is for the reader to "play it safe" and assume that the relationship is a fairly close one. In such cases, the reader usually feels obliged to read the cover letter with far greater care than if the letter were sent by someone not having a personal connection with the organization.

The lesson here should be clear. If you have a personal connection with the company to which you are writing, by all means use it in the opening paragraph of your letter. It will all but guarantee that your letter will be read.

In those cases where you are particularly interested in working for a specific employer and know no employees whom you can reference in your introductory paragraph, try cultivating such a contact within the company. This can normally be done with a little research and some creative networking. Here are some ways you can accomplish this.

1. *Industry Association Networking*   Using an industry association membership roster, identify key persons who, by title, would appear to be employed by your target firm in positions that are closely related to your field. Call these individuals, introduce yourself, and engage in some conversation about the company (e.g., products, markets, competition, strategy). You are now in a position to quote these people on the basis of these conversations.

2. *Professional Association Networking*   Join one or two professional associations and search the association membership roster for members currently employed by your target company. As with industry association networking, call these individuals and engage them in conversation about the company (its products, markets, competitors, management philosophy, strategies, job opportunities, etc.). Here again, you have made a contact you can quote in the introductory sentence of your cover letter.

3. *Literature Search*   If you can't identify employees through either a trade or a professional association membership roster, try doing so through a literature search. Using the computer facilities of a local library, try searching periodicals for articles that reference your target company. Many times, such articles will quote company employees whom you can contact. Using the articles you've found as the basis for initial discussion with these employees, you can soon lead the discussion toward topics of more immediate concern to your job search.

As you can see, it is relatively easy (with a little imagination, some basic research, and a simple telephone call) to develop a valuable contact at a target firm. Once you have talked with an employee, it is also a relatively easy matter to discover some ways of using the information obtained as ammunition for the lead sentence of your cover letter.

Here are some ways you can effectively introduce this personal contact at the beginning of the cover letter:

During recent discussions with Steve Temple, your Manager of Accounting, I became aware of your concern about the need to automate the Accounts Payable function. Perhaps I can be of help.

Sandy Slagle, your Director of Marketing, was telling me that you may be looking for a Manager of Public Affairs. I am interested in talking with you about this position.

I have recently learned from Jane Swanson, your Director of Total Quality, about the work that you are currently doing in research with experimental design. As a Senior Research Statistician at Exxon's Research Center, this is a subject with which I am intimately familiar.

I recently learned from John Brighton, your Manufacturing Manager, that you are looking for a Senior Industrial Engineer. On the basis of John's description of some of the challenges that this position will face, I would be very interested in discussing this opportunity with you.

As you can see from these examples, in each case, there is a specific employee mentioned in the very first sentence of the introductory paragraph. Because of this "personal contact" type of introduction, it will be very difficult for the reader not to read the cover letter. Most will feel obligated to read it in the event that, at some future point, the referenced employee inquires about the letter and/or the author's employment status.

If you are unable to identify an employee to reference, another technique to generate reader interest is to make use of specific company knowledge. As with the "personal contact" technique, this serves to personalize the letter and take it out of the mass-mailed, broadcast category.

Sample B at the end of this chapter is an example of a cover letter that employs specific company information in the first paragraph as an interest generator. Most employers are impressed by a letter that shows an applicant has taken time to research the company. This is in sharp contrast to the hundreds of mass-mailed letters received by the employer in which it is evident that the prospective candidate knows little or nothing about the company.

If it is evident in the cover letter that the applicant has taken the time to research the company and personalize his or her letter, most employers will reciprocate by investing some time in reading it. The fact that the letter's author was sufficiently interested in employment with the company to do some research usually elicits very positive feelings on the part of the employer and serves to create a sense of obligation to read the cover letter with greater care and attention than that given to the mass-mailed, impersonal variety.

Sample B demonstrates effective use of this technique by a college student applying for a position as an accounting trainee. Notice how the student not only references the firm's college recruiting literature, but also uses the opening paragraph to relate this literature to her own job interests. In most cases, this sort of introduction will generate interest and compel the employer to read the rest of the cover letter.

Likewise, sample C makes use not only of personal contact but also of specific company knowledge. In this letter, Sandra Jackson advises Craig Deters, President of United Chemicals, that she has learned that the company is seriously considering implementation of a Deming-based "total quality" program and may be in the market for someone to lead this effort. Deters is likely to be somewhat surprised by and impressed with Sandra's knowledge of his plans. As a result, he is highly likely to read all of Jackson's cover letter.

Here are some additional examples of introductory paragraphs that employ specific company knowledge to generate reader interest:

I read the article concerning Champion Corporation's use of modern organization development techniques in the August 2 issue of Business Week. *As a seasoned O.D. professional, I found this article unusually interesting, and it has prompted my decision to apply for employment with your company.*

The recent article in the TAPPI Journal *concerning Phillips Paper's decision to undertake a $1.2 billion capital expansion of its Mobile paper mill suggests that you may be in the market for experienced paper machine project engineers. If this is the case, you are likely to have an interest in my background.*

Some recent research that I have done on your company reveals that in the last three years Cooper Technologies has taken the leadership *in the field of asbestos abatement. The fact that your sales have gone from $8.2 million to over $40 million during this same period is most impressive. I would like to be affiliated with your company.*

I recently read several articles concerning Dansforth Corporation's research advances in the field of transparent electrophotography. The electro-scanning technology used in this process is truly revolutionary and exciting. I feel that my work as a photo-imaging scientist closely parallels your research and that, as a result, you may have some interest in my qualifications for employment with your company.

Each of these introductory paragraphs makes very effective use of the specific company knowledge technique. There is a very specific reference to some aspect of the company (e.g., growth, products, technology) that makes it quite evident that the applicant has taken the time to acquire some first-hand knowledge of the company. This conveys a level of personal interest the employer sees infrequently and serves to set you apart from the everyday job seeker who applies to the company using an impersonal, mass-mailed broadcast letter. The net result is to generate a heightened interest on the part of the letter's recipient that is usually sufficient to warrant full reading of the cover letter.

As mentioned earlier, another technique that can prove effective in generating reader interest in your cover letter is using a compliment in the introductory paragraph. Most employees have some pride in the company for which they work. A complimentary remark normally appeals to this sense of pride and thus creates interest in your cover letter. The warm feelings you have created may well carry the reader through the rest of your cover letter and reflect positively on your candidacy.

One caution about the use of the compliment technique! If you elect to use a compliment, make sure that it is genuine and truly reflects your feeling about the company. Nothing turns an employer off more quickly than an insincere compliment. Such insincerity is normally easily spotted.

Most employers are insulted by insincere flattery. They feel that it is an insult to their intelligence for the writer to think that he or she could employ such a sham and expect to get away with it. The best rule to follow here is, if you don't believe the compliment, don't use it.

While working in the executive search profession, we often received cover letters that used insincere flattery. It appears that certain outplacement or career consulting firms are counseling job seekers to employ the complimentary technique in their cover letters to executive search consulting firms. Some examples of wording frequently employed by the clients of these firms are:

An acquaintance of mine, whose judgment I respect, has highly recommended your firm as one of the outstanding executive search firms.

A colleague of mine has told me of your excellent reputation as an executive search firm that specializes in the recruitment of financial executives.

I recently learned about the reputation of The Bradford Group in the real estate industry. Several associates have told me about the high quality and reliability of your work in real estate search.

A colleague, whose opinion I respect, mentioned your quality search work in sales and marketing.

Although, on the surface, these complimentary openings may seem both innocent and genuine, they are not. The problem is that I have received hundreds of cover letters using almost the exact same wording. Additionally, since we were a generalist firm that does not focus on or specialize in a particular area, it is quite obvious that people using these "canned" introductions had no direct knowledge of our firm. Thus, these introductions ring with insincerity and do little to increase the desire to read further.

The key word, then, in the use of the complimentary cover letter introduction is "sincerity." If you use a compliment, make sure it comes across as genuine and sincere.

Sample cover letter D uses the complimentary introduction. It compliments Mr. Wilson as someone who is "aware of the importance and value of a top flight Chief Financial Officer." Naturally, Mr. Wilson would like to think of himself as having this kind of awareness; so the compliment serves to hook his ego and will likely generate sufficient interest to motivate him to read on.

Some other examples of how the complimentary introduction might be used to generate reader interest follow:

Because of the Shallinsworth Company's fine reputation as a market leader in the field of microwave electronics and its excellent reputation as an employer concerned with the development of its employees,

I am interested in pursuing the possibility of employment. Accordingly, I am enclosing my resume for your review and consideration.

During my last five years as Sales Representative in the industrial fastener industry, I have watched Wilco Corporation's market entry and rapid rise to its current position as industry leader. Needless to say, your company's growth has been quite impressive. I would like to be a part of this growth and feel that I can further strengthen your market presence in the Southwest. Enclosed, therefore, please find my resume for your consideration.

Ever since I entered the field of pharmaceutical research in 1986, I have admired the quality of Benson Laboratory's work in the field of cardiovascular research. As a research scientist with over twenty patents and a reputation for creativity in the same field, I would appreciate the opportunity to explore the possibility of a position as a member of your respected research staff.

I recently read your article on Barnsworth Company's commitment to the participatory management concept, and I was quite impressed. I have long been an advocate of the participatory management concept and firmly believe that it is the only way to unleash and capitalize on an organization's full human resource potential.

Your comments have piqued my interest, and I would therefore appreciate the opportunity to discuss how I might assist Barnsworth to further capitalize on this exciting concept as an internal O.D. consultant to the company.

I have long admired The Wadsworth Company's excellent reputation as a market leader in the field of specialty chemicals. Mr. Baskerville, as the Director of Market Research for a company that enjoys such market preeminence, you must, I am sure, derive a great deal of professional satisfaction from your work and the contributions you have made to your employer as its marketing leader. I am fascinated with the idea of being part of a marketing research organization such as yours, and would welcome the opportunity to explore this possibility during a personal interview.

As you can see, using the complimentary introductory paragraph can be quite effective in generating reader interest in your cover letter and resume. The personal nature of these complimentary remarks, in most cases, will ensure that your letter is read by the employer, increasing the possibility of a subsequent interview.

Again, of the three interest-generating techniques described here, the most effective is the use of personal contacts. Both specific company knowledge and the complimentary introduction, however, can also serve your purpose rather nicely. All three are a substantial improvement over the typical introductory remarks found in most mass-mailed cover letters, and can provide you with the competitive edge you will need to get the employer's attention and increase the possibility of landing that all-important interview.

Value-Selling Paragraph

Another key characteristic of effective cover letters is the use of the "value-selling" paragraph. This is the paragraph that describes the value you can bring to the hiring organization and that provides the basis for motivating the employer to invite you for an interview.

A well-written value-selling paragraph is not simply a sterile listing of your strengths. Instead, it lists specific results achieved and contributions made in other firms and states or implies that you can make similar contributions to the prospective employer's firm as well. The inference that will normally be drawn by the prospective employer is that you are someone who is capable of adding value to his or her organization. You already have a track record that demonstrates this.

Modern interview theory subscribes to the principle that the best predictor of future performance is past performance in the same or similar areas. This is the basis for behavior-based interviewing. Employers are looking for tangible evidence of the ability to do certain things. Thus, the candidate's capabilities and qualifications are normally judged by specific results achieved in certain key areas thought to be critical or important to good job performance.

The purpose of the value-selling paragraph, therefore, is to facilitate the employer's evaluation process. By citing results achieved in areas thought to be critical to good job performance, you are providing tangible evidence of your ability to perform in these important areas and, thereby, to add value to the organization.

Usually, the dilemma faced at this juncture by most cover letter authors is deciding which specific results to highlight. Which ones will be truly value adding from the employer's perspective? Unfortunately, many job seekers ignore that question and choose to highlight those contributions of which they are most proud, with little regard to the probable needs of the employer. This is a serious mistake!

If you are tempted to do this, you need to go back to basics. One of the fundamental mistakes made by most salespersons is to begin lauding attributes of the product or service he or she is selling without first understanding the specific needs of the customer. Hence, the salesperson will drone on and on, covering information that is of little or no real interest to the customer. The end result is loss of the sale.

Successful salespersons, on the other hand, have always known that the sale must be focused on customer needs. What motivates one customer to buy may not motivate another. One may be looking for price; another, quality; another, ease of operation; another, time savings; another, cost savings; another, aesthetics; and so on. Not determining and qualifying these needs in advance may result in emphasizing product attributes that are not important to a particular customer. Even worse, it may cause the salesperson to neglect key product attributes that would more than satisfy the customer's needs and result in a sale.

An analogy can be drawn with selling your attributes in the cover letter. If you are to create an image of yourself as someone who can be value adding and who can contribute in areas important to the employer, you must first start with an understanding of the employer's needs—those key areas where he or she is likely to be looking for improvement. When determining this, ask yourself these questions:

1. What key problems is the employer looking to solve?
2. What similar problems have you successfully solved? What were the results?
3. What is the organization's long-term strategy?
4. What changes will it need to bring about in order to achieve these strategic goals?
5. What new problems will need to be solved to realize these strategic objectives?
6. What similar problems have you successfully solved? With what results?
7. What new methods or technology is the employer attempting to apply? For what purpose?
8. How have you applied such methods or technology? With what results?

Ideally, to write a highly effective value-selling paragraph, you should use your networking contacts within the target company to research these questions in advance of designing your cover letter and resume. The answers will allow you to tailor these documents to the specific needs of the employer, thus stacking the deck in your favor and substantially increasing your chances of a successful outcome. I would strongly recommend that you do this for the dozen or so target companies for which you would most like to work. It will have substantial payoff!

In cases where the remaining number of target firms is simply too large to warrant individual research, I suggest that you sort them into industry groupings and then conduct some good industry research. Some important questions to keep in mind when performing such research are:

1. What are the major problems confronting this industry?
2. What knowledge and skills are required to solve problems?
3. What are the major trends and changes being pursued by companies within this industry?
4. What new knowledge (e.g., methods, technology, techniques) is required to facilitate these changes?
5. What specific knowledge, skills, and capabilities do you possess that will enable you to:
   a. Solve these major industry problems?
   b. Orchestrate these desired changes or trends?
6. What evidence can you cite of your overall capabilities in these important areas (i.e., results achieved, contributions made)?

By answering these and similar questions, you will automatically develop the ammunition for writing a good value-selling paragraph that is focused on the key needs of the target industry. These needs, of course, will reflect the individual needs of many of the organizations in each industry grouping. You are once again stacking the deck in your favor by appealing to the specific needs of most of these member companies. This should serve to substantially increase the odds for a favorable result.

The four sample cover letters at the end of this chapter provide examples of value-selling paragraphs. Each paragraph, as you will see, focuses on the ability of the author to contribute something of value to the employer. Note that it is not simply a delineation of the candidate's strengths; each paragraph focuses on his or her ability to make specific contributions that will in some way prove beneficial to the hiring organization.

The value-selling paragraph provides a key opportunity to market yourself to prospective employers and to motivate them to act favorably on your employment candidacy. If carefully thought out and well-written, this paragraph can make a significant difference in the effectiveness of your cover letter and result in many more interview opportunities. It must be well-written, however, and, to maximize effectiveness, must be focused on the real needs of the employer. Perhaps no other paragraph is more important to cover letter effectiveness.

Background Summary

In reviewing the sample cover letters at the end of this chapter, you will note that another characteristic they exhibit in common is use of the background summary. The background summary provides a brief synopsis of your relevant education and experience. Usually, it includes the academic degree held, major field of study, number of years of experience, and a short description of job-relevant experience.

The purpose of this summary is to convey to the employer that you have the appropriate training, experience, and seasoning to support the position for which you are applying. Keep this summary brief, since it is intended to be only a short synopsis of relevant education and experience and is not intended to replace the full resume that accompanies the cover letter.

Action Statement

Any expert in the field of advertising and promotion will tell you that for a sales letter to be effective, it should contain an action statement that somehow ensures action beyond simply reading the letter. Your cover letters should include a statement that urges the employer to take favorable action on your employment candidacy or that tells the employer that you intend to take action by calling to determine interest and, if appropriate, arrange for an interview.

Examples of action statements from the cover letters at the end of the chapter are shown on page 49.

I will plan to call you next week to determine if you are interested in discussing this matter further and, if appropriate, to arrange for a meeting with you.

I would appreciate the opportunity to discuss how I might further contribute to the Dixon Company's research efforts through a personal interview. I will call you on Tuesday, March 28, to determine your interest and, if appropriate, to arrange for a personal meeting.

I would be pleased to have the opportunity to interview with your college recruiting representative during your January recruiting schedule, and hope that you will give the enclosed resume favorable consideration.

Should you be in the market for a top flight financial officer who can add profits to your bottom line, I would appreciate hearing from you.

Here are some additional examples of action statements for your consideration:

I will plan to call you on the afternoon of September 30 to determine your interest and, if agreeable, to arrange for a personal meeting.

I will call your office on Wednesday, January 15, to determine your interest and a suitable time for a meeting with your recruiter.

Should you have an appropriate opening in your Research Center, I would welcome the opportunity to meet with you personally. I can be reached at (315) 455-7224 during the day and (315) 467-9951 during evenings and weekends. I look forward to hearing from you.

Although this may prove too time consuming and impractical if you are currently employed, wherever possible, you should take the initiative by offering to call the prospective employer. In this way, there is nothing left to chance. Besides politely forcing the employer to take action on your candidacy, this technique has the advantage of providing you with a contact for further networking, even if the employer has no further interest in your candidacy.

Statement of Appreciation

The final hallmark of a good cover letter is courtesy. Since most employers are very busy people, you should express your appreciation for the time they are taking to review and consider your employment credentials. A simple statement of appreciation will suffice.

The following are some examples of statements of appreciation:

Thank you for your consideration.

I appreciate your consideration of my credentials, and look forward to hearing from you.

I hope that you will give the enclosed resume favorable consideration. Thank you.

Thank you for your consideration. I look forward to hearing from you shortly.

Although one or more of the elements discussed in this chapter may be missing from a given letter, my experience has convinced me that these are the basic characteristics contained in most effective cover letters. Letters that are well designed for maximum effectiveness, in my judgment, should thus attempt to incorporate all of them.

SAMPLE A   *Good Cover Letter*

250 East Windsor Lane
Perryville, OH 17375
June 15, 1998

Mr. Edward T. Ressler
Vice President of Technology
Reardon Corporation
22 Technology Circle
Malvern, PA 19348

Dear Mr. Ressler:

Statement of Interest

I am writing to express my strong interest in employment as a Senior Statistician in the Technology function of Reardon Corporation. To this end I am enclosing a complete resume outlining my professional qualifications for your review and consideration.

Value Selling

You may be interested to know that my qualifications should enable me to add immeasurably to the overall efficiency and productivity of Reardon's research efforts through the application of various statistical methods. By training your scientists in statistically-based experimental design, laboratory experiments can be executed with much greater accuracy and predictability. Through consulting support in such areas as variance analysis, I can also help your technical staff to identify, isolate, study and understand those variables critical to process performance and product quality. This translates to faster, more dependable research results and millions in cost savings!

Background Summary

My credentials include a Ph.D. in Applied Statistics and over 15 years research experience. I am thoroughly versed in a wide range of statistical methods including: design of experiments, variance analysis, regression analysis, process capability studies, statistical process control, etc.

Compelling Action

I would appreciate the opportunity to discuss further the specific contributions I could make to Reardon Corporation through a personal interview. I will call within the next couple of days to determine your interest and, if appropriate, to arrange for a personal meeting at your convenience.

Statement of Appreciation

Thank you for your consideration.

Sincerely,

Barbara D. Briggens
Barbara D. Briggens

bdb

Enclosure

SAMPLE B   *Good Cover Letter*

133 Overlook Ridge
Whitetail, CO 13726
December 12, 1997

Ms. Linda A. Cooper
Corporate Accounting Manager
Wasserman Company, Inc.
233 Commerce Drive
Denver, CO 15672

Dear Ms. Cooper:

*Use of
Company
Knowledge
& Statement
of Interest*

Your college recruiting literature states that you hire Accounting Trainees as entry-level employees in the Corporate Accounting function. The idea of having rotational assignments in auditing, tax compliance and cost accounting sounds extremely interesting to me. I am therefore interested in interviewing with your firm during your forthcoming recruiting trip to the University of Colorado.

*Value
Selling*

I will graduate with a B.S. degree in Accounting in June of next year. I have been a strong student and have been recognized by the University for my academic achievement through receipt of various awards and scholarships, which are detailed on my enclosed resume.

*Value
Selling*

In addition to my academic accomplishments, you will note that I have always been very industrious and hard working. As my resume will attest, I have been continually employed either full or part-time, since age thirteen. Despite this work schedule, I have also managed to squeeze in a healthy slate of extracurricular activities, showing an ability to effectively plan and manage my time.

*Value
Selling*

My solid academic performance, strong work ethic, drive, organization skills, and passion for the accounting field will hopefully convince you that I have the basic ingredients to make a valuable contribution to Wasserman Company's Accounting function.

*Statement of
Appreciation*

I would be very pleased to have the opportunity to interview with your campus representative during your January recruiting trip to our school, and I hope that you will give my candidacy favorable consideration. Thank you.

Sincerely,

David S. Rothwell

David S. Rothwell
Student

dsr

Enclosure

SAMPLE C   *Good Cover Letter*

122 Government Drive
Falls Church, VA 17264
August 25, 1998

Mr. Craig C. Deters, President
United Chemicals, Inc.
300 East Market Street
Baltimore, MD 18237

Dear Mr. Deters:

Use of
Personal
Contact

During a recent conversation with your Director of Manufacturing, Walt Stevenson, I was advised that you are considering implementation of a Deming-based "total quality" program at United Chemicals, and may be in the market for a strong leader to direct this effort. Should you be seeking such a leader, you may well want to consider my credentials for this assignment.

Background
Summary

A Ph.D. in Statistics with over fifteen years in the field of quality management, I have thorough training in Deming's management principles and am skilled in such statistical methodology as experimental design, process capability studies, variance analysis, statistical process control, etc. I am a Fellow of the American Statistical Association and enjoy national recognition in my field.

Value
Selling

Important to your needs, I have provided overall leadership to a highly successful corporate-wide total quality initiative at Wilson Chemical which is credited with substantial ($100 million) improvement to business performance this year alone. I would welcome the challenge of undertaking a similar effort at United.

Compelling
Action

I will call you next week to determine if you are interested in discussing this matter and, if appropriate, to arrange for a meeting with you.

Use of
Compliment

I have heard some excellent things from Walt about your leadership at United, and look forward to the possibility of meeting you personally.

Sincerely,

Sandra E. Jackson

Sandra E. Jackson

SEJ:mmr

Enclosure

SAMPLE D   *Good Cover Letter*

24 Willow Spring Road
Dayton, OH 13058
May 20, 1999

Mr. William F. Wilson
President & Chief Operating Officer
Martin Science, Inc.
315 Technology Place
Walnut Creek, CA 12847

Dear Mr. Wilson:

Use of
Compliment

As the senior executive of a leading U.S. technology company, I know that you are aware of the importance of having a top flight Chief Financial Officer to handle the financial challenges of a growing enterprise. If you are in need of such an individual, you may want to consider my credentials.

Background
Summary
and
Value
Selling

A financial executive with over fifteen years in electronics manufacturing, I have logged some significant successes in such important areas as low-cost capitalization of major expansions and acquisitions, significant cash flow improvement, debt reduction, improved credit standing, and overall profit enhancement. In my current position, I recently led a corporate-wide cost reduction effort that contributed nearly 30% profit improvement in the last year alone.

Reason for
Job Search

Despite this success, I find it necessary to seek a new employment relationship. As a family-owned enterprise, my current employer offers little hope for further career growth and enhancement.

Compensation
Requirements

Current compensation is $135,000 plus bonus, and my requirements are in the mid $100,000 range. The opportunity for some participation in ownership, through stock options or outright "buy in", is important to me at this stage of my career.

Compelling
Action and
Statement of
Appreciation

Should you be in the market for a results-driven senior financial executive, who has a solid history of delivering significant additions to the corporate bottom line, I would appreciate hearing from you.

Sincerely,

Wellington J. Baxter

wjb

Enclosure

4

CHARACTERISTICS OF POOR COVER LETTERS

We learned in the preceding chapter that there are certain common characteristics of good cover letters. These characteristics are:

1. An "interest-generating" first paragraph that grabs the reader's attention.
2. A "value-selling" paragraph that focuses on employer needs and demonstrates the ability to solve key problems and drive desired strategic change.
3. A "background summary" paragraph that highlights relevant education and experience.
4. An "action-compelling" statement that either compels or ensures follow-up action.
5. A statement of appreciation.

Elements of Bad Cover Letters

It should stand to reason that poor letters are generally characterized by the absence of one or more of these important elements. But, although this is certainly true, there are other factors that can account for the lack of impact and effectiveness. The focus of this chapter will be on these additional characteristics that contribute to overall cover letter ineffectiveness. They are:

1. Poor overall appearance.
2. Poor grammar, punctuation, and misspelled words.
3. Rambling—lack of focus.
4. Self-focused versus employer-focused.
5. Bland, boring text.
6. Gross exaggeration—bragging.
7. Aggressive, pushy tone.
8. Self-deprecation.

Let's examine each of these detracting characteristics is detail, so that you can more fully appreciate the impact they have on cover letter effectiveness. To facilitate this, I have included sample cover letters that exhibit these undesirable elements. The chapter is arranged so that a corresponding sample immediately follows discussion of each of these negative factors.

Poor Overall Appearance

Sample A represents a cover letter that exhibits poor overall appearance.

Perhaps the most frequent transgression of cover letter authors is to cram too much information onto the page. Sample A is a typical example of this. Note how the text is pushed out against the left and right margins of the letter, leaving almost no white space as a neat frame. This contributes to an overall congested appearance and detracts substantially from the letter's effectiveness.

Careful review of this sample also reveals that it does not fully conform to acceptable cover letter format, as discussed in Chapter 2. Although it generally follows the standard block format, its complimentary close and signature line should not be flush with the left hand margin, but should be positioned in line with the return address and date line at the top. Further, Mr. Stewart's title is missing, and there is no space provided between the salutation and the first line of the initial paragraph. In addition, the signature has been crammed against the bottom of the page so that there is no room to include a typed signature line immediately below Simpleton's signature.

This departure from acceptable format contributes to the letter's poor appearance, detracting from both the aesthetics and general balance of the letter's layout.

Failure to provide space between paragraphs causes the text to flow together and makes it somewhat difficult to read. Space between paragraphs would have set them apart and would have substantially improved both appearance and readability.

Also detracting from the overall appearance of this letter are the many misspelled words, typographical errors, and resultant manual corrections to the text. Although you would expect to see this kind of thing on a first or second draft, it should never appear on the final copy that is sent to an employer. All such changes should be made on the draft, and the final document should be flawless.

When a cover letter of this sort is received by a prospective employer, the impression created is a very poor one. It suggests that the candidate who has sent it is careless and sloppy. Most employers will not even bother to read such a poorly prepared letter and will simply move on to the next candidate.

SAMPLE A   *Poor Cover Letter*
(Poor Overall Appearance)

120 Flatstone Drive
Phoenix, AZ 17264
June 30, 1998

Mr. Douglas C. Stanton
Wellington Corporation
250 Industry Avenue
Braintree, MA 26385

Dear Mr. Stanton:

I am writing to you to ask for a job. There are many good reasons for you to consider my candidicy, and I think you would find it werth your time to meet with me. I am quite a good salesperson.

I attended Hillsboro University where I earned an degree in Marketing Management. I followed gratuation with the position of Sales Representative at Random Company, where I recieved the Presidents Award as top salesperson.I nearly doubled saales during my two years at Random, but was unhappy with my compensation level and resigned to take a position with Quick-Fix Tool Company in Atlanta, Georgia.

While at Quick-Fix Tool, I served as Regional Sales Manager for the Northeast Region and covered Maine, New Hamshire, Vermont, Massasschusetts, and Upstate New York. In 1993, the territory was enlarged to include Connecticut and Rhode Island as well. In this capacity I managed the sale of industrial grade power tools to retail stores and contracters, increasing annual sales by five percent for each of the three years I was there. Dissattisfaction with continual product quality problems forced me to leave Quick-Fix for a position with Robotool in 1995

I am currently National Sales Manager with Robotool and manage a 85 person salesforce, with responsability for worldwide sales of power tools to industrial and commercial accounts. Sales, which totaled $50 million in 1997, are through lisensed dealers and a global network of manufacturers representatives.In the last two years, we have made significant penetration into the Europen market and have also expanded sales to both Russia and China. Strategies that I have emplementd during my tenure at Robotool have resulted in increased sales of over 50 percent.

My experience includes over nine years selling power tools to retail,industrial and contractor accounts. I have successfully managed salesforces of 10 to 85 representatives on a regional, national and global basis. I have taken and taught numerous sales courses, and have a strong comittment to development of people. I am described as "high energy" and am considered to be highly motivated.

My current income exceeds $150,000, and is comprised of a base salary of $120,000 and bonus of over $30,000. I would require a comparable compinsation package, along with company car, expenses, insurance bebefits, and stock options. Additionally, I would like to limit travel to no more than 70 percent of the time.

I hope that I will hear from you soon, and that we will have the oppertunity to personnally meet to discuss how I can help you to achieve your marketing and sales goals. I know that you would find such a meeting very benifical.

Very respectfuly yours,

SAMPLE B   *Poor Cover Letter*
(Poor Grammar, Punctuation, and Misspelled Words)

125 North Arlington Drive
Buffalo, NY 18736
May 15, 1997

Ms. Katherine Wainscott
Director of Manufacturing
Fahrling, Inc,
235 West River Drive
Macon, GA 12847

Dear Ms. Wainscott:

I seen your newspaper add in the New Yoak Times for a managar of Manufacturing Services
at your Lawndale Ohio plant. I am interested in this position very much and would
appreceate the oppurtunity to interview for this here position.

My perfessional background includes a B.S. degree in Business Administration from
Enlightened University plus more then seventeen years experence in manufacturing
management. Of particular interest should be the fact that I werked for your competitor The
Phillips Company as the Manager of Manufacturing for neerly six years.

Some of my major akomplishments include:

- Decreased manufacturing costs by allmost 30 percent thru installation of new
  skeduling system.

- Started up new steal bolt manufacturing line 3 weeks ahed of skedule with
  compleetly trained crews.

- Installed Just-In-Time inventory system that redused inventory capitol investment
  by more then 25%.

I know that I can make a reel contribution to your company and I feel that you should give
serous concideration to hiring me. Lets us plan to get together to talk about the perspects of
my employment with your company. I will plan to call your offise next Wednesday to see if
I can skedule a meeting to xplore the possability of a mutual intrist.

Thank you for your concideration.

Sincerely,

Norman N Numbskull

Norman N. Numbskull

Poor Grammar, Punctuation, and Misspelled Words

Sample B depicts a cover letter that is loaded with misspelled words and poor punctuation and grammar. Although the letter is neat and well designed, the reader's initial positive impressions of the candidate are, unfortunately, quickly dispelled once he or she begins to wade into the text.

Poor grammar, bad punctuation, and misspelled words suggest that the applicant is either poorly educated or simply doesn't care about the impression created. If he is applying for a position that requires good verbal and written communication skills, the author of this letter, Mr. Numbskull, has done little to endear himself to the prospective employer. The chances are unusually high that the employer is going to forgo reading the accompanying resume and quickly move on to the next job applicant.

Few things can turn an employer off more quickly than poor English. If you are not particularly adept in this area, I strongly suggest that you have a knowledgeable friend proofread your cover letter very thoroughly before going to press.

Rambling—Lack of Focus

A rambling cover letter can suggest to a prospective employer that the author is unfocused and generally disorganized. Such a letter is represented by sample C.

You will note, in reviewing sample C, that a major contributing factor in its nonfocused, rambling style is the use of unnecessary words. As an exercise that should help you avoid writing this kind of letter, try editing the sample letter, removing all words that do not add information or enhance meaning. Next, try rewriting each sentence of the remaining text more concisely. Can you convey the same thoughts with fewer words? With a little effort, you'll be amazed at the results you get.

Although sample C contains a lot of information, this information is not presented in an organized, meaningful, and compelling way that motivates the employer to take action. It would appear to be simply a summary of the applicant's background that does little to focus on selling the employer on the value the author can add to the firm. It is a bland recital of the writer's education and employment history with a few random thoughts thrown in concerning personal traits and philosophy. And none of it is woven together particularly well.

SAMPLE C   *Poor Cover Letter*
(Rambling—Lack of Focus)

1604 Willard Avenue
Dallas, TX 12948
September 23, 1997

Mr. David R. Rawlins
Director of Public Affairs
Kennsington Corporation
20 Canal Street
Austin, TX 19283

Dear Mr. Rawlins:

I am very interested in the possibility of employment with your company, and I am therefore submitting my resume for your review and consideration. I think you will find my background very interesting. Please consider my qualifications for any suitable opening you may have currently available in the Public Affairs function of your firm.

I hold a B.A. degree in Communications from Intelligentsia University, where I excelled as an undergraduate student. While at the University I was awarded the Koehler Award for my many contributions to the community and remain, to this day, heavily involved with community service of one kind or another.

I am considered quite an outgoing, friendly person by those who know me well. When asked to describe Ron Rambling, most of my friends would probably use such adjectives as open, honest, sincere, loyal, dedicated and hard working. I have always been very dedicated to my work and loyal to my employers. I am well motivated and am capable of carrying out my work assignments with little or no supervision.

Following graduation from Intelligentsia, I spent three years in the Peace Corps, where I learned the true meaning of life through giving to others. I came to appreciate the small things of life and the value of personal relationships. These basic values have served me well in the business world, as I have pursued my career goals and objectives.

My work history encompasses nearly twelve years in the field of Public Affairs. Most recently, I have been Manager of Contributions for the Ballinger Company, a $3 billion manufacturer of consumer products. In this capacity, I have managed an annual contributions budget of $1.2 million. I have also spent nearly three years as Ballinger's Customer Services Supervisor, a position that I enjoyed thoroughly.

Thank you for your consideration, Mr. Rawlins, and I look forward to hearing from you.

Sincerely,

Ronald R. Rambling

Ronald R. Rambling

Rambling letters will not promote your employment candidacy and can, in fact, negatively affect your efforts. Try to design letters that are concise and well focused in support of your stated job objective.

Self-Focused versus Employer-Focused

Sample D depicts a letter that is self- rather than employer-focused. There is little in this letter that will convince the employer of the candidate's ability to add value to the hiring organization.

This letter clearly focuses on the needs of the applicant. It describes the reason for her job search, the type of position sought, the organizational culture sought, and compensation requirements. She does nothing to address the needs of the employer.

Bear in mind that employers hire people because of their ability to add value to the organization. They are not interested in the applicant's demands but in his or her ability to solve key problems, help achieve strategic objectives, apply state-of-the-art methods, and so forth.

A self-focused cover letter that does not address your capability to make meaningful contributions to the firm falls considerably short of its primary purpose. It will do little to convince the employer that there are good reasons to interview you. Instead, it will create an impression that you are self-centered and concerned only with your own needs, and it will not help you win the all-important employment interview.

Bland, Boring Text

Sample E is an example of a cover letter that employs bland and boring text. Unfortunately, it is all too typical of the cover letters received by employers and executive search firms.

Generally, this type of letter is characterized by a bland presentation of educational credentials and an unexciting summary of professional work experience. Moreover, there is no attempt to relate these credentials to the needs of the target organization. Such letters also tend to be verbose, containing a lot of unnecessary words that add little to the information presented in the accompanying resume.

A bland, boring letter does not excite the prospective employer's imagination. It tends to suggest that the author lacks creativity and resourcefulness—the very traits toward which most employers gravitate when looking for persons who can bring fresh new ideas, solve key

SAMPLE D   *Poor Cover Letter*
(Self-Focus versus Employer-Focused)

200 Cindy Drive
Raleigh, NC 18236
October 20, 1998

Mr. Sean R. Brennan
Vice President of Operations
Z-Wave Electronics, Inc.
100 Silicon Way
Brighton Beach, FL 18775

Dear Mr. Brennan:

A recent downsizing at Carlton Electronics has resulted in a 40% layoff of salaried staff. My former position as Manufacturing Manager—Printed Circuits has been eliminated, and I am now forced to seek other employment.

My goal is a position in manufacturing management with a medium- to large-sized electronics manufacturing company. I prefer working for a growth-oriented company where the prospects for sustained, long-term growth appear excellent. I also seek a position offering well-defined advancement opportunity to senior level management in the intermediate (i.e., three- to five-year) term.

The company I am seeking will be a strong advocate and practitioner of the "participative" style of management. It believes that the proper role of a manager is that of a teacher, coach, facilitator—an enabler of others. This company is committed to management through others rather than to the management of things.

My compensation requirements are in the low $100,000 range, with the opportunity for salary review and increase on an annual basis. I also require a comprehensive benefits package.

To arrange for an employment interview, please contact me at (413) 775-9424. I look forward to hearing from you shortly. Thank you.

Sincerely,

Cynthia A. Selflove

Cynthia A. Selflove

cas

Enclosure

SAMPLE E   *Poor Cover Letter*
(Bland, Boring Text)

105 Seaview Road
Portland, OR 19274
April 16, 1999

Mr. Willard P. Pennysworth
Manager of Corporate Accounting
The Blakely Group, Inc.
200 Financial Plaza
Boston, MA 18726

Dear Mr. Pennysworth:

I am writing to you for the purpose of applying for the position of Cost Accountant with The Blakely Group, Inc. I have enclosed a copy of my personal resume for your review and consideration. I trust that this resume will contain all of the information that you will need to make a proper assessment of my employment credentials; however, should you require any additional information, please advise me and I will be pleased to furnish whatever additional data you require.

As you can see from the enclosed employment resume document, I earned a B.S. degree in Accounting from Washington State University, where I graduated in 1992. Following graduation from Washington State, my professional career began with Price Waterhouse, where I worked as an Auditor for four years. I resigned from Price Waterhouse in 1996, to accept employment as a Cost Accountant with the Hauptbrau Company at their Portland Plant. I have now worked for Hauptbrau for almost three years, and I have recently decided to seek employment elsewhere.

I have been a solid employee for my past employers. I have had excellent work attendance and have missed only four days of work in the past seven years. Additionally, I have been a good performer, and I can furnish both personal and business references should this be required.

I am currently earning $75,000 per year with Hauptbrau, and my next salary review is due in July of this year. My annual increases have normally been in the 3 to 5% range. My minimum salary requirements with a new employer, therefore, are in the $78,000+ range.

Please review the enclosed employment resume and let me know if you have any appropriate openings that are a match for my qualifications and interests. Thank you for your consideration.

Respectfully yours,

Brandon B. Boring

Brandon B. Boring

bbb

Enclosure

problems, and help the firm to achieve competitive advantage in the marketplace. Such lack of imagination will certainly not distinguish you from the masses and will likely cause the prospective employer to move on to other more resourceful applicants.

Employment cover letters need to convey a certain sense of excitement and enthusiasm. They need to demonstrate that the author is alive, alert, resourceful, creative, and anxious to make a valuable contribution to his or her next employer. Bland, boring cover letters hardly accomplish this objective.

Gross Exaggeration—Bragging

Another mistake too often made by many cover letter authors is to cross over the fine line between emphasizing strengths and outright bragging. Sample F crosses this line and thus reflects poorly on the author.

Generally, the most common cause of a letter's bragging tone is the overuse of superlatives, which tends to make the writer appear insincere and prone toward exaggeration. The result is an aura of being "bigger than life," and the employer thus begins to question the applicant's credibility. There is also a clear demarcation between bragging and exaggeration, or lying.

Most employment experts agree that it is important to "toot your own horn" in the employment process. You do need to emphasize your strengths, accomplishments, and attributes in a positive and engaging way. It is important, however, that you do so in a socially acceptable way and that you not lose credibility with your audience. If you fail to use good taste in tooting your own horn, your cover letter can be very damaging (or even fatal) to your employment campaign.

If you suspect that you may be coming across too strongly, have someone critique your letter for tone. Ask if it sounds as if you are bragging and request assistance in choosing words that will tone things down a bit but still help you to make your point.

Aggressive, Pushy Tone

Tone is very important to the effectiveness of your cover letter. Although you want to be assertive and motivate the reader to take appropriate action, be careful that you don't come across as too aggressive or pushy.

Sample G is an example of an aggressive, pushy letter. The tone of a letter crosses the fine line between assertiveness and aggressiveness

SAMPLE F   *Poor Cover Letter*
(Exaggeration—Bragging)

235 Meadowbrooke Road
Wilmington, DE 13859
May 21, 1998

Ms. Karen A. Winslow
Vice President Marketing and Sales
Heatherwood Industries, Inc.
900 Revenue Drive
Williamsport, PA 19326

Dear Ms. Winslow:

As Vice President of Marketing and Sales for a well-known and highly successful manufacturing
company, I'm sure that you recognize a talented salesperson when you see one. That is precisely
the reason you need to get to know me! Should this event occur, I am sure that you will agree
that I am one of the most talented and capable salespersons that you have had the opportunity to
meet.

My record will show that I have consistently been one of the top producers for each of my past
employers. Not only am I an exceptional sales talent, but I am known for being intelligent, bright,
outgoing, high-energy, and tenacious. I never miss landing the order! My past employers have
often marvelled at my ability to consistently turn in top flight performance.

As testimony to my superior sales skills, you should know that I have never gone through an
employment interview without receiving a job offer. It seems that once they meet me, all
employers want to do is to have me on their sales team. My ability to make a significant
contribution is self-evident!

It should be obvious to you that an employment interview is warranted, and that we should meet
to explore what Heatherwood Industries can offer an outstanding prospect like me. I will await
your call and can be reached at (302) 664-9173.

I expect to hear from you shortly.

Sincerely,

Barbara B. Braggart

Barbara B. Braggart

bbb

Enclosure

SAMPLE G   *Poor Cover Letter*
(Aggressive, Pushy Tone)

320 Wayland Drive
Oklahoma City, OK 82175
October 22, 1998

Mr. Walter F. Jensen
Vice President of Logistics
Space Industries, Inc.
20 East Commerce Highway
San Diego, CA 18274

Dear Mr. Jensen:

I am applying for the position of Corporate Distribution Manager at Space Industries. I have excellent credentials, and I am sure that you will be impressed with my accomplishments, as set forth on the enclosed resume. Read this document carefully!

I hold an M.B.A. in Materials Management from the University of Oklahoma, where I graduated in 1993. My undergraduate degree is in Industrial Engineering from the same school. In both instances I was an outstanding scholar, graduating with honors and serving in leadership roles in several student organizations.

My professional credentials include over six years in the field of Logistics. This includes over two years as Distribution Manager for General Electronics, a Fortune 200 manufacturer of computer chips and electronic harnesses, with annual sales of $5.3 billion. I am thoroughly versed in all aspects of modern distribution methods, and can bring state-of-the-art skills to your firm.

Let me suggest that even if you don't have a current opening on your management team, that you may want to meet with me anyway. A meeting will show that I have the kind of potential that may warrant some organizational shifts to make room for me as a valued member of your staff. We can discuss the specifics of title and compensation requirements at that time.

I will call you on Wednesday, October 28th to arrange for an interview. Convenient dates for me include November 7th, 14th, 18th and 21st.

I expect that we will be meeting shortly!

Sincerely,

Priscilla P. Pushy

Priscilla P. Pushy

rap

Enclosure

when the language that is used becomes offensive to the reader. In sample G, the sentence "Read this document carefully!" is clearly offensive. It is an order rather than a request.

When writing a cover letter, as when writing any other business letter, you must always consider the tone in the context of the relationship between the author and the recipient. If that relationship is vendor and customer or job applicant and employer, it is important that the writer show appropriate respect for the recipient. Violating this relationship by telling the recipient what, how, or when to do something will not endear you; so be careful to avoid this tendency when writing your employment cover letter.

Here again, it is a good idea to read your letter for tone before sending it. Place yourself in the employer's shoes. How would you feel if you received this letter? Is there any wording that you would find offensive? If so, it's time to edit!

It is also a good idea to have someone else read your letter for tone. Sometimes, because you are the author, it's hard to see the forest for the trees. You may simply be too close to the work to pick up the subtleties of tone. If you cross that fine line and insult or offend the reader, you can be sure that another good employment opportunity has just gone by the wayside.

Self-Deprecation

Some employment candidates have a facility for using the employment cover letter for "shooting themselves in the foot." Sample H is an excellent example. I call this tendency "self-deprecation."

One mainstay of the self-deprecating cover letter is the author's compulsion to point out that he or she falls short of the needed employment qualifications. Our sample cover letter does a great job of this.

Another characteristic of the self-deprecating letter is the tendency for the author to come across as shy and somewhat apologetic, as if he or she has no right to be applying for the targeted position. There is a tendency also to sound overly appreciative of the reader's consideration. Such tendencies make the candidate seem wimpish and without self-confidence—two traits of which the employer will take special notice.

It is important that you come across as someone who is confident and self-assured. It is also important that you be seen as well qualified to get the job done. Pointing out your shortcomings, acting subservient, and being wimpish will certainly not serve this purpose.

SAMPLE H   *Poor Cover Letter*
(Self-Deprecation)

16 Miller's Place
Waldon, TX 18274
March 20, 1997

Ms. Judith R. Linderman
Manager of Public Affairs
Dorrie Manufacturing Company
800 Industry Avenue
Nashville, TN 28372

Dear Ms. Linderman:

I would very much like to apply for a position as a Regional Lobbyist with Dorrie Manufacturing Company. I hope that I have the necessary qualifications to be considered for this position.

Although I lack a college degree, and my written communication skills are not as good as they could be, I hope that you will give consideration to my employment candidacy. I am a hard worker and do my best to accomplish the objectives of my employer.

I would be very pleased if you would look favorably on my employment candidacy. I want this job very much and would work very hard if selected. I know that I am not fully qualified for this position, but I hope that you will give me a chance to demonstrate how well I can do.

Although there are likely others whose education and experience make them better qualified for this position, I still hope that you will view my resume favorably. I hope to hear from you soon.

Thank you very much for taking the time and effort to read my resume. I appreciate this very much.

Sincerely,

Timothy T. Timid

Timothy T. Timid

ttt

Enclosure

5

ADVANCE PREPARATION

As with preparing to write the resume or getting ready for the interview, solid preparation for writing an effective cover letter will clearly have a significant impact on the final outcome of your job search. If you have not taken time to prepare, your letter will likely have little meaningful content and may suggest to the reader that you are disorganized and shallow thinking.

I am frequently amazed at how much time and energy are committed to writing an effective resume, while little if any thought is given to the construction of an effective cover letter. Yet, it is almost always the cover letter that first greets the eyes of the prospective employer. It is the cover letter that either makes the sale or loses it.

Nothing kills a job search faster than a poorly prepared cover letter! If it is poorly designed, disorganized, uninteresting, full of grammatical errors and poor spelling, and so forth, in many cases the employer will not even bother to go on to the resume, but will frequently consign both letter and resume to the "no interest" pile and move on to the next cover letter in the stack. The pity of this is that the candidate may have excellent employment credentials, which are prominently displayed on the resume, however, the employer never even bothered to go beyond the cover letter.

By contrast, a well-written cover letter will capture the reader's interest and convince him or her that the applicant has something of value to contribute to the organization. If the letter is well constructed, the reader will feel a heightened curiosity and read the accompanying resume with interest. In fact, if particularly well-written, the cover letter may, in some cases, convince the reader to interview the candidate without reviewing the attendant resume. This is, admittedly, a rare occurrence; however, it is possible.

You should think of the cover letter as you do of your appearance if you are going to meet someone you hope to impress. In this case, you will want to commit sufficient preparation time to ensure that you make a good presentation. You will want to select just the right suit or dress and accessories. Your scarf or tie will need to be just the right color and texture to complement your outfit. Your shirt or blouse will need to be clean, crisp, and well ironed and your shoes, well shined. Your hair will need to be neatly groomed and your fingernails clean and well manicured. Everything will need to be just right to make a very favorable first impression and ensure that the relationship gets off to a good start.

Why should the cover letter be any different? Since it serves to introduce you to the employer, isn't it just as important that it be well written to ensure that this initial introduction is a favorable one? The answer to this is obvious. Why, then, do so many people short-cut the cover letter writing process? I'm not really sure of the answer to this question. I do know, however, that many do short-cut this important step, and the results are frequently disastrous!

A well-written cover letter doesn't just happen. It is the product of solid advance planning and painstaking care. It is the end result of careful thought and analysis that serves to relate your specific skills and capabilities to the requirements of the position you are seeking.

The Preparation Process

In order to write an effective cover letter, the job applicant must go through three steps. These are:

1. Job target analysis.
2. Self-analysis.
3. Qualifications comparison.

Let's take a few moments to explore each of these important steps, which make up the "overall capability audit."

Job Target Analysis

Since an effective cover letter will need to focus on your qualifications for the job for which you are applying, it would seem to make good sense that your cover letter preparation process start with a detailed analysis of this job. In particular, you will need to know what specific knowledge and skills will be needed for successful performance. You can bet the ranch that these are the same factors that the employer will be looking for when scanning your cover letter and resume. Why not make the employer's job easier right from the start by highlighting these same factors in your cover letter!

Here are some questions that should help you with this job analysis step. Fill in the answers as you go.

1. What are the key functions performed or managed by this position?

_____

_____

_____

_____

_____

_____

2. What are the key ongoing functional accountabilities of this posi-
    tion (i.e., the key results expected for each function)?

_____

_____

_____

_____

_____

_____

3. What are the key problems that must be solved to achieve these
    functional results?

_____

_____

_____

_____

_____

_____

4. What specialized or technical knowledge is required to solve these problems and achieve the expected functional results?

   A. Fields
   B. Disciplines
   C. Laws/principles/theories
   D. Functions

   E. Methods/procedures
   F. Technology
   G. Equipment
   H. Processes

   _____

   _____

   _____

   _____

   _____

   _____

Completion of the job analysis step should ensure that you are now focusing on the specific knowledge that will be required for this position. The next step in the cover letter preparation process is self-analysis.

Self-Analysis

Now that you have completed the job analysis, your next objective should be to carefully examine your background and experience to determine how well your specialized knowledge compares to the knowledge requirements of your targeted job. When completing this step, it is important to keep in mind that such knowledge is acquired in two ways:

1. Through formal education.
2. Through experience.

You must therefore carefully examine both your formal education and your professional experience to determine how this knowledge was acquired.

It is not enough simply to determine that you have the prerequisite knowledge to solve the key problems for which you will be held accountable. Employers will want to see evidence that you are able to apply this knowledge effectively and that you have achieved favorable results in the past. In behavioral interview terms, the employer will want to see behavioral evidence of your ability to achieve favorable results in those areas thought to be critical to successful job performance—that is, evidence that you are capable of successfully solving the key problems with which you will be confronted if hired for the position.

In order to successfully carry out this self-analysis step, you will have to systematically examine each facet of your background and experience to determine:

1. Key job-related knowledge that you possess.
2. How this knowledge was acquired.
3. Evidence of your ability to apply this knowledge.
4. Key results that have been achieved through application of this knowledge.

The following forms are designed to help you organize the self-evaluation process.

Education

In the spaces provided below, fill in all information requested, starting with your most recent degree.

Degree: _____ Major: _____
What specific knowledge did you acquire that should help you solve the key problems and achieve the key functional results required of this position?

_____

_____

_____

_____

_____

Degree: _____ Major: _____

What specific knowledge did you acquire that should help you solve the key problems and achieve the key functional results required of this position?

_____

_____

_____

_____

_____

_____

Training

Beyond your formal education, what additional training courses or seminars have you attended that have provided you with job-relevant knowledge in those areas previously identified as critical to successful job performance?

Course/seminar attended: _____

Key knowledge acquired: _____

_____

_____

_____

_____

Course/seminar attended: _____

Key knowledge acquired: _____

_____

_____

_____

_____

Course/seminar attended: _____

Key knowledge acquired: _____

_____

_____

_____

_____

Use additional paper, if required, to complete this analysis of your relevant training courses and seminars. Be sure that you are concentrating only on those that have helped you develop specific knowledge that is important to solving the key functional problems for which you will be accountable in your target position. Avoid any training that is not relevant to this position.

Work Experience

Analysis of your professional experience, in most cases, will be the most important part of the self-analysis process. It is here that you will have the opportunity to identify your specific achievements and results in those functional areas for which you will be accountable in the new position. Such accomplishments provide convincing evidence to prospective employers of your ability to solve important job-related problems and achieve required functional results. They provide tangible proof of your ability to be "value adding" to the new organization.

To start this process, review past positions you have held to determine which are most closely related to your target job. Which of these positions have had the same or similar functional accountabilities as those in the target position? Which have required you to solve problems similar to those you will face in the new position? Include in your analysis only those having functional accountabilities and problems similar to your target position. Nonrelated positions should be skipped.

Complete the following information for each relevant position:

Position Title: _____

Company: _____

Division: _____

Department: _____

Key functional accountabilities: _____

_____

_____

_____

_____

_____

Key functional results achieved: _____

_____

_____

_____

_____

_____

Time in position: _____

Position title: _____

Company: _____

Department: _____

Key functional accountabilities: _____

_____

_____

_____

_____

Key functional results achieved: _____

_____

_____

_____

_____

Time in position: _____

Position title: _____

Company: _____

Department: _____

Key functional accountabilities: _____

_____

_____

_____

_____

_____

Key functional results achieved: _____

_____

_____

_____

_____

_____

Time in Position: _____

Use additional paper if you need more space to complete this analysis.

Analysis of your relevant work history should provide you with an excellent list of target job related accomplishments from which to choose as you begin to design your cover letter. Because you have taken the time to complete the analysis, this information will be at your fingertips when you need it.

Qualifications Analysis

I am sure that having completed both the position analysis and your self-analysis, you have become keenly aware of many specific examples of how your education, training, and experience have prepared you to carry out the functional responsibilities of your target position and achieve the key functional results that prospective employers will expect of you. More important, if you have been thorough, you have likely identified significant results that you have achieved that offer convincing evidence of your ability to solve the key functional problems confronted by these prospective employers. Citing such achievements in the cover letter can be a powerful tool in persuading employers of your ability to be a major value-adding contributor to their organizations. It can form the very heart of an effective cover letter.

After the position analysis and self-analysis, the next step in the cover letter advance preparation process is the qualifications comparison. The intent of this process is threefold:

1. To determine where your qualifications and the requirements of the target position overlap.
2. To determine the functional priorities of target companies.
3. To allow you to select those achievements having greatest positive impact on these functional priorities.

The following set of questions should help you with this process and allow you to narrow the field down to those achievements that will have the most favorable impact on the companies you have targeted for your job search.

1. Of the various functions for which your target position is responsible which are probably the most important from the standpoint of overall organizational success? (Arrange these in order of organizational impact.)

_____

_____

_____

_____

_____

2. What are the desired functional results required for overall organizational success for each of the previously listed priority functions? (List these results in the same order.)

_____

_____

_____

_____

3. Using the self-analysis data previously developed, list the most significant results you have achieved that correspond to the desired functional results listed in Question 2.

_____

_____

_____

_____

_____

You have now completed your overall capability audit and have developed the kind of information you will need to design effective cover letters. This should save you considerable time as it becomes necessary throughout your job-hunting campaign to write various kinds of cover letters. It will allow you to quickly identify and highlight those qualifications and accomplishments most related to the critical functional needs of the employer. These are the ones that will do the most to promote your job search interests by positioning you as a key contributor in those areas most important to organizational success. This approach is sure to convince most employers that you have what it takes for successful job performance and that your employment candidacy is well worth pursuing.

6

COVER LETTER
INCLUSIONS/EXCLUSIONS

What kind of information should be included in the cover letter? Or, perhaps as important, what information is better left out? This is one of the frequent dilemmas faced by the cover letter author.

If you were recently laid off, should you offer an explanation in the cover letter? If you have held several previous jobs with numerous employers, should you offer an explanation for your frequent movement? Should you attempt to explain employment gaps in your resume? How about physical handicaps or serious health problems? Should these be discussed in the cover letter?

These and similar questions are the topic of this chapter. We will attempt to provide you with some guidelines for answering them and for deciding what type of information is truly beneficial to the objectives of the cover letter and your job search. Conversely, we will also discuss criteria for deciding what kind of information may detract from cover letter effectiveness and thus should best be excluded. Let's examine these categories one at a time.

Job Objective

Generally, it is felt that a statement of your employment interest including job objective, should be included in the first paragraph of the cover letter. This conveys to the reader the intent of your letter and serves to focus his or her attention on your qualifications. Here are some examples of introductory paragraphs that include a job objective statement:

Enclosed please find my resume for your review. I am interested in applying for a position as purchasing agent with Barron Chemical, and would appreciate your consideration of my employment credentials.

I am seeking a responsible position in R&D management requiring a Ph.D. with 15 years of experience and proven skills in polymer and specialty chemical research.

As President of a leading firm in the electronics field, you are aware, I am sure, of the importance and value of a top flight Chief Financial Officer. If you are seeking such an individual, you may wish to give serious consideration to my credentials.

If you do not include a statement of your job objective near the beginning of the cover letter, you will fail to focus the reader's attention on the reason for your letter. To simply state that you are interested in employment, without specifying your job objective, can leave the impression that you are vague, indirect, or indecisive, or all three. It may also suggest to the employer that you are somewhat desperate for employment and, consequently, will accept any old thing. These are certainly not the impressions that you want to create in your cover letter.

On the other hand, the inclusion of a job objective in the beginning paragraph adds focus to your cover letter. It helps to establish the reason for your letter and focuses the reader's attention on your credentials for such an assignment. It also suggests to the employer that you are organized, direct, focused, and businesslike in your approach. These are far more desirable descriptors.

In stating an employment objective, however, you should be particularly careful in choosing your words. If the objective provides too narrow a description, it may cause you to be screened out from consideration for positions that may, in fact, be of interest to you. If described too broadly, on the other hand, the objective may suggest that you are vague and indecisive. Here are some examples:

I am seeking a senior-level accounting or financial position with broad management responsibility for achievement of the company's financial objectives.

I seek a position with responsibility for overall direction of the financial planning function.

I am looking for a good career position with your organization.

The first objective is worded rather broadly and suggests that the candidate is receptive to a wide range of financial and accounting positions (including financial planning). The second objective is a bit more confining and limits employment consideration to financial planning only. This suggests that the candidate would not consider other related financial and accounting positions, thus serving to screen him or her out from consideration for such positions. Finally, the third objective is unusually vague and fails to provide the desired focus necessary to an effective cover letter.

You can see from these examples that the wording of the objective statement is of considerable importance. You will need to word your statement with great care so that you focus the reader's attention but don't screen yourself from opportunities that you may wish to consider.

Reason for Job Search

Some cover letter authors feel compelled to offer the employer an explanation for their job search. This is particularly true if their separation from their last employer was the result of a layoff or company downsizing program.

Many writers include such an explanation in response to what I call "historical guilt." In the old days (i.e., 15 to 20 or so years ago), there was social stigma attached to being unemployed. Unemployment suggested that you were unstable, lazy, unreliable, and otherwise unable to hold a job. If you had been previously employed, current unemployment, in many cases, also suggested that you may have been fired. As a result, people who were legitimately laid off felt compelled to differentiate their circumstances from the "socially undesirable" by offering an explanation for their employment separation. Today, this is no longer the case.

The continuing rash of corporate downsizings throughout the United States has served to separate a number of good performers from the corporate ranks. Many of these downsizing efforts have included "voluntary" programs offering various financial incentives for voluntary resignation from the company. Some of these programs have offered up to a year's pay or more to encourage employee resignation—often sufficient incentive to allow frustrated but otherwise good performers to gracefully exit the organization.

The ranks of the unemployed today contain a number of good workers, and most employers are well aware of this fact. There is, therefore, considerably less social stigma attached to being unemployed, and employers are less likely to associate unemployment with laziness, instability, or poor performance. Unless the period of unemployment has been of considerable duration (i.e., a year or more), therefore, you should not feel compelled to offer an explanation in the cover letter. If you feel that you "must" do so, however, here are some ways to accomplish this.

A recent decision by the Baxtor Corporation to shut down its Wexler Division has necessitated my current job search.

I have recently elected to participate in Darrow Corporation's voluntary separation program for the purpose of pursuing more promising career options.

As a key executive in the appliance manufacturing field, you are aware, I am sure, of Brighton Corporation's decision to close its Wayne Narrows Plant. As a consequence of this decision, I am currently seeking a responsible position as a Director of Manufacturing.

In general, unless you feel compelled to do so, I recommend that you not include such explanations. Since the purpose of your cover letter is to sell the employer on the idea of interviewing you, such explanations are seldom beneficial to this objective. To the contrary, they tend to take up valuable space that might be more constructively used to market your skills and overall capability. I believe that the issue of past job separations is usually better handled at the time of the employment interview.

Explanation of Employment Gaps

If your resume contains employment gaps, you may or may not want to use the cover letter to provide an explanation. Generally, however, unless there is an acceptable reason for these gaps, such explanations are best left out. They only serve as a "red flag" that draws the reader's attention away from your positive qualifications as an employment candidate. Why highlight this potentially negative information in your cover letter?

I would also not attempt to explain employment gaps in the resume. Why make it easy for the employer to spot them? At least, by excluding this information, you may have the opportunity to discuss the matter during the employment interview. By then, however, you have also had an opportunity to counter this potential negative by effectively marketing your ability to make contributions to the hiring organization. Should you volunteer an explanation of these gaps in advance, you may never even have the opportunity for an interview with the employer.

So, in final analysis, my recommendation is, don't volunteer this information—let the employer ask.

Compensation

Should you list compensation history or compensation requirements in the cover letter? It all depends upon the circumstances.

Generally, the inclusion of salary information does not add much to the cover letter. And it can serve to focus the reader's attention on cost rather than on the value you can bring to the organization. This is particularly true if your current pay level is considered high for your position, background, and years of experience. Sensitivity, of course, diminishes if your current compensation level places you in the lower level of a prospective employer's salary range.

Another argument against including salary information in the cover letter relates to the space it requires. Due to the limited space available in the cover letter, it is generally felt that this same space might be more effectively used to market your qualifications and overall value.

Another factor to consider, when determining whether to include salary information, is your current employment status. If you are comfortably employed and are in a position to wait until just the right opportunity comes along, there is a lot less to lose if you are screened out because of salary requirements. In such cases, you may want to state your requirements in the letter, since this could serve your interests by screening out lower-paying opportunities that do not fit your needs.

On the other hand, if you have been unemployed for a lengthy period of time and are feeling somewhat desperate, listing your salary requirements in the cover letter could screen you out from opportunities that you might later wish you had pursued. By excluding salary information, you may at least afford yourself the opportunity to find out more about the position with a prospective employer. Armed with information not only about the immediate opening but also about such things as future advancement opportunities and the company's benefits program, you could well be happy that you didn't allow yourself to be screened from consideration.

Sometimes people whose salaries are particularly low by comparative standards may feel that listing their compensation level in the cover letter will induce employers to pursue their candidacy. Although this may work in some cases, in others, it may backfire. For example, an unusually low salary can be a red flag to certain employers, causing them to question just how competent and qualified the candidate is. Obviously, there must be something wrong!

The general rule of thumb suggested by most employment experts is, don't volunteer either salary history or compensation requirements in the cover letter unless specifically asked by the employer to furnish this information. Even in those cases where you have been asked to state compensation requirements, try to avoid being too specific. In responding to such requests, it is usually best to cite a range—for example, mid-$70K range or low-$80K range. By doing this, you are not automatically screening yourself out, and you are still preserving some flexibility for future salary negotiations.

Employer Hopping

The job hopper is someone who simply has had too many employers in too short a time. Should the job hopper use the cover letter to offer some explanation for the number of moves made? Let's explore this question in some detail.

Although there is no set standard, it is well known that having too many jobs in too short a time can be very detrimental to a job search. What might be considered an excessive number of employers in one industry, however, may be considered average in another. For example, those who work as engineers for engineering job shops or contract engineering firms are frequently subject to layoffs. If the economy is healthy and firms are engaged in hefty capital expansion projects, engineering contractors can't get enough engineers. On the other hand, when the economy contracts and capital expansion dries up, it's layoff time.

Firms engaged in contract engineering and similar industries that are heavily affected by swings in the economic cycle are accustomed to seeing several moves on an individual's resume. But industries that are less volatile would expect to see fewer employment changes. So, what constitutes the job stability standard in one industry may be totally different from the standard in another.

Further confusing this topic is the fact that there are many reasons why an individual changes employers. Some of them are considered "acceptable" in the eyes of the employment professional; others are deemed "unacceptable." Here are some examples:

Acceptable Reasons

1. Elimination of job.
2. Elimination of function/department.
3. Company-wide layoff.
4. Voluntary resignation as part of downsizing.
5. Company acquisition and subsequent layoff.
6. Nepotism—replaced by relative of owner.
7. Health.

Unacceptable Reasons

1. Poor performance.
2. Incompatibility with management/fellow workers.
3. Absenteeism.
4. Dishonesty.
5. Quitting without notice.

Although it should be obvious that you should not use the cover letter to highlight unacceptable reasons for past terminations, how about those cases where such termination was for acceptable reasons? Should this information be volunteered in the cover letter to distinguish you from those who have been involuntarily terminated for unacceptable reasons?

In general, regardless of reason, it is recommended that the job hunter not use the cover letter to offer explanations for job hopping. This only highlights the problem and detracts from the candidate's presentation of overall skills and capabilities. In fact, if the job applicant can do a sufficient job of marketing his or her ability to add value to the organization, the prospective employer may be willing to overlook past transgressions. Instead of highlighting these past moves in the cover letter, therefore, I recommend that the problem of job hopping be dealt with in another medium—namely, the resume.

The problem can be best addressed by choosing a resume format that emphasizes skills and accomplishments and deemphasizes employment chronology. Thus, the job hunter should choose a functional rather than a chronological resume format. A well-prepared functional resume will focus the employer's attention on skills and accomplishments rather than on periods of employment. For further information on how to prepare an effective functional resume, you might want to consult my book, *The Resume Kit,* Fourth Edition (Wiley, 2000).

Experience Deficit

If you lack prerequisite experience to qualify for your job objective, should this lack be addressed in the cover letter? My advice here is similar to that offered in the discussion of job hopping.

By using the cover letter to discuss the fact that you do not possess the prerequisite experience required for a given position, you are substantially detracting from your employment candidacy in the eyes of the employer. Why highlight this fact in the cover letter, giving the employer every reason to screen you out? Why not let the employer discover this independently? Why make it easy and destroy whatever chances you might have had to convince the employer that you are a candidate worth considering?

If you think about the fundamentals of the employment decision-making process from the employer's viewpoint, you will likely conclude that the employer is hiring someone on the basis of ability to solve certain key problems and make certain key contributions—not on the basis of past experience. The focus is therefore on whether you possess certain knowledge and skills and can effectively apply them to the areas of concern to the prospective employer. Although not frequently, I have witnessed employers totally abandon specific experience requirements in the interests of hiring a particular candidate who, they felt, had excellent skills in those areas critical to successful job performance.

With this in mind, don't jeopardize your chances for employment by highlighting your lack of specific experience in the cover letter. Instead, use the cover letter to effectively market your skills and capabilities (as well as your desire and motivation) to make substantive contributions to the employer.

Here again, the functional resume format can be used, in conjunction with the skills-focused cover letter, to reinforce your qualifications for the position you seek. This format, rather than the chronological resume format, will enable you to focus the employer's attention on your overall skills and capabilities rather than on past work experience. The skills-focused letter and the functional resume, in combination, can complement each other nicely, providing some pretty convincing evidence of your potential for successful job performance.

Educational Deficit

For purposes of our discussion, the term "educational deficit" means a lack of the educational qualifications normally required by most employers when filling a given professional position. Most employers attempting to fill an engineering position will require a degree in engineering; likewise, when filling a position in market research, most will require an M.B.A. in marketing. Many other examples could easily be cited where the requirement for certain educational credentials might be considered ironclad.

As with an experience deficit, it is recommended that you not attempt to explain away a specific educational deficit in your cover letter. It is generally best that it not be mentioned in the cover letter at all— why underline it by volunteering its existence? What real purpose does this serve? If anything, it will likely screen you from consideration before the employer has had a chance to review your other qualifications in the accompanying resume. This is particularly important when you have had direct experience in the field for which you are applying and can, as a result, graphically demonstrate your ability to successfully perform the job.

Under these circumstances, it is far more important to use the cover letter to focus the reader's attention on specific accomplishments and results achieved that are directly related to the position for which you are applying. You can thus provide a convincing argument supporting your ability to make valuable contributions to the hiring organization. For most employers, this is far more important than the specifics of one's educational background.

Sure, your candidacy is somewhat handicapped by not having the specific educational credentials normally sought for such positions. But this may be far from fatal depending upon what evidence you can cite concerning your ability to meet the major requirements of the position. After all, knowledge is acquired by means other than formal education. It can just as easily be acquired through informal training and actual job experience. Job experience, in particular, can provide invaluable education that has benefits far beyond those normally acquired in the formal classroom. After all, it is the actual job environment that tests your ability to apply your knowledge. Simply having the formal education is not enough if you are unable to successfully apply what you have learned.

So, in final analysis, you should avoid bringing this educational deficit to an employer's attention in the cover letter. Furthermore, when designing the resume that will accompany your cover letter, be sure to obscure your educational credentials by listing them near the bottom of the second page rather than prominently displaying them at the beginning. I have seen many highly successful people who, on the basis of their educational credentials alone, would not survive the employment screening process.

Physical Handicap or Serious Illness

If you have a physical handicap or a chronic serious illness, should you mention this fact in the cover letter? This is not an easy question to answer and requires a bit of discussion.

Generally, the guidelines I recommend for making this determination are related to two things:

1. The severity of the condition.
2. Your level of social confidence.

If the severity of your condition is such that it would have little bearing on your ability to perform the job in question, my advice is clear: Don't bring the subject up in your cover letter. Instead, assuming you feel compelled to bring this to the employer's attention at all, wait until the hiring process has proceeded to the point that the employer has made clear his or her strong interest in you. It is at this point that your condition is least likely to have a negative impact on your chances of being hired. The employer is already convinced that you have what it takes to successfully contribute to the organization and will be more likely to overlook this issue than if confronted with it at the outset of the screening process.

If you are suffering from a chronic condition that will clearly affect your ability to perform the job, again, I would not mention this fact in the cover letter, especially if some sort of reasonable accommodation can be provided (i.e., special desk, chair, device) that will allow you to function normally. Unfortunately, such mention will, in many cases, automatically screen you from further consideration.

Here again, it is better to wait until the interview to address this topic. At least you will have gained the opportunity to present your credentials and convince the employer that you can be a valuable contributor despite your handicap or medical condition. If you are successful in marketing your overall qualifications and capabilities during the interview, perhaps the conversation can then turn to providing the necessary support and accommodations you need to sustain your job performance at a consistently high level.

An important consideration when deciding whether to mention your handicap in the cover letter is your level of social comfort. If you are fairly comfortable with your handicap and will not be embarrassed by the interviewer's potential surprise or awkwardness, by all means, do not mention your handicap in the cover letter. On the other hand, if you are severely handicapped and feel compelled to advise the employer of this, then do so.

Should you elect to discuss your handicap or medical condition in the cover letter, be sure to provide sufficient information. Don't keep the employer guessing about your ability to perform the job. This discussion should give a fairly detailed and accurate description of your physical limitations and how they relate to your ability to function.

Don't overdo it, however. Remember, the employer is really interested in your job qualifications. It is important, therefore, that you offer a convincing presentation of your qualifications and your interest in the job. First generate interest in your candidacy, and then, having accomplished this, introduce the subject of your handicap, along with a frank description of your limitations and some convincing evidence showing that they will not substantially affect your ability to perform the major duties of the job for which you are applying.

I hope this chapter has answered most of your important questions concerning the kinds of information that should be included in or excluded from your employment cover letter. Some of these matters are rather delicate and will require careful handling if you are to put your best foot forward and end up with that critical employment interview. Carefully consider the content of your cover letter, therefore, to be sure that you maximize your opportunities for presenting your case to the employer on a face-to-face basis. Be sure not to include unnecessary topics that may screen you out before you even have a chance to get started.

7

GENERAL BROADCAST COVER LETTERS

The general broadcast cover letter is the kind of letter used by the job seeker to mass-mail his or her resume to a large number of prospective employers. Although commonly used, the direct mail campaign is not known to be a highly productive employment technique. In a successful direct mail campaign, the response rate will normally run in the 2 to 5 percent range. Most employment candidates should consider themselves quite fortunate to realize this kind of response. However, there are times when, with a well-designed cover letter and resume, response rates can be quite a bit higher.

Probably, the single factor accounting for the low level of response from the direct mail campaign is competition. It is not uncommon for the corporate employment department of a major corporation, for example, to receive 40,000 to 50,000 resumes a year. Some of the more sought-after large corporations, in fact, are known to receive well over 100,000 employment inquiries a year.

Compounding this problem of volume competition has been the "skinnying down" process many employers have gone through in recent years. In an effort to become more cost competitive, they have substantially cut the size of their workforces. Cuts in the 20 to 30 percent range are not uncommon, with staff functions such as the employment department being reduced by as much as 50 percent. To handle the large volume of unsolicited employment inquiries with smaller staffs, many employers are now outsourcing this activity to outside contractors.

Given the volume of employment inquiries received by these employers, coupled with substantially reduced staffing of their employment departments, it is not difficult to understand why the direct mail campaign is not a highly productive job-hunting technique. If read at all, unsolicited employment inquiries receive only a cursory review. There is simply not the time or the manpower to warrant a more thorough approach.

This does not mean that you should avoid using the direct mail approach as part of your job search. To the contrary, this technique is considered to be a standard in every well-planned employment campaign. Although it requires considerable work for the level of anticipated result, it should be kept in mind that just one favorable response resulting from a well-orchestrated direct mail campaign has the potential to provide you with an excellent job offer and an exciting career opportunity. Due to the low response rate, however, it should not be considered the cornerstone of your employment strategy.

Target Companies

It is not uncommon for employment candidates to target several hundred companies for their direct mail lists. Sometimes, they may include as many as 500 or more. However, the direct mail list usually consists of what I call the "second tier" companies. It should not include the 10 or 20 "primary" target companies for which you would most like to work. These companies should be singled out for a much more tailored, customized approach (including individual research) than that offered by the general, broadcast type direct mail campaign.

The number of companies included in the target list for the broadbased direct mail campaign makes it impractical to conduct individual company research; so the cover letter used is less focused and must be designed to appeal to a much broader audience. It will not be possible to design a single letter that addresses the specific needs of such a large list of employers. A different tack is required here.

Generic Results

Since the number of companies to be included in the direct mail campaign is simply too large to allow a tailored, needs-focused approach, the cover letter will need to be more generic. By this I mean that it must be designed to appeal to the generic, or common needs of all companies.

As discussed earlier, employers don't fill jobs just for the sake of filling them. Instead, they expect to fill their openings with persons they think are capable of achieving certain results and thereby adding value to the organization. Therefore, good cover letter design requires that the letter, as well as the accompanying resume, highlight your ability to contribute specific results to the prospective employer's organization.

A mere summary of your education and employment history does not really accomplish this. Such a summary simply states your general qualifications; it doesn't highlight the contributions you can make and the value you can bring to the firm. To be persuasive and convince an employer that you are someone worth pursuing, you will need to focus the employer's attention on the kind of results that can be expected if you are hired. The best way to do this is to use the cover letter to highlight some of the key results you have accomplished for employers in the past.

If you are looking back over a number of years of employment, you may find it difficult to decide which past results to highlight. The best way to make this decision is to determine which are most relevant to the type of position for which you are applying. Here are some questions that may help you with this process:

1. What are the key generic responsibilities of the position for which you are applying?
2. If these responsibilities are met, what specific results would you expect to see?
3. What similar job responsibilities have you had in the past?
4. What were the major results and accomplishments you achieved in these key areas of responsibility?

In answering these questions, you will likely find that the kind of responsibilities and results identified are fairly common, or generic to the job function. These appear to be universal, regardless of the employer. Here are some examples of what I mean:

Function:	*Manufacturing*
Key accountability:	Produce highest quality product at lowest possible cost.
Valued results:	Increased quality. Reduced scrap. Reduced costs (labor/material). Increased output.
Function:	*Marketing*
Key accountability:	Increase sales volume and market share with minimum investment and maximum return.
Valued results:	Increased sales volume. Increased market share. Increased penetration—existing market. New market penetration. Reduced advertising expense.
Function:	*Human Resources*
Key accountability:	Increase organizational productivity through improved planning, selection, development, and motivation of employees.

Valued results:	Reduced employee turnover.
	No labor strikes.
	Improved employee attendance.
	Reduced work-related injuries.
	Increased production per employee.

As you can see, these valued results are generic. They are universally expected of the occupational specialty in which one works, regardless of the employer or the employer's work. These are common results that all employers consider highly desirable; so if you choose to highlight them in a general broadcast cover letter, you will be focusing on values that have universal appeal.

Review of the sample cover letters at the end of this chapter will reveal that these results or contributions can be presented in either linear or paragraph form. Sample A is an example of the linear approach. Here, each key result or accomplishment is highlighted on a separate line. Sample D, on the other hand, highlights these accomplishments in paragraph form. In my judgment, the linear approach is more effective, since each accomplishment is presented on a separate line and is therefore more visible.

Skills and Attributes Focus

A recent graduate, who has no prior relevant work experience, will not be able to cite specific work-related accomplishments. In such instances, a different approach is required in the cover letter. He or she can emphasize specific technical skills and personal attributes thought to be important to good job performance. Cover letter sample B is an example of such an approach.

In sample B, Phillip Jones, an upcoming graduate of Bucknell University, is using his cover letter to apply for a position as a sales trainee with The Clawson Company. Since Phillip has no appropriate sales experience, he chooses to highlight personal accomplishments and attributes that he feels are important to good performance as a sales professional. Some of these are:

- Interest and enthusiasm.
- Outgoing, friendly personality.

- Enjoy developing strong personal relationships.
- Bias for action.
- Strong service orientation.
- Drive and determination.
- Leadership.
- Energy.

Phillip's letter is particularly well-written, and it serves to relate some of his personal attributes to specific results desired of good sales professionals.

Cover Letter Elements

Review of the sample cover letters at the end of this chapter suggests that there are certain elements that are common to most general broadcast letters that are used for employer mailings. These are:

1. Block or full block format.
2. Address of a specific hiring executive.
3. Introductory paragraph including statement of objective.
4. Statement of relevant accomplishments.
5. Brief background summary.
6. Request for action.
7. Statement of appreciation.

Let's take a few moments to discuss each of these elements so that you can fully appreciate their role in and their overall importance to the effectiveness of your cover letter.

As is the case with other cover letters discussed in this book, the formats recommended for the general broadcast cover letter are block and full block. Both are widely used and accepted designs that increase ease of reading and present an overall neat, organized appearance. These formats are discussed in great detail in Chapter 2, so I will not discuss them further here.

You will note that each of the sample letters in this chapter is addressed to a specific executive by both name and title. In each case, he or she has broad management responsibilities for the function in which the job applicant has interest, and is normally also responsible for making hiring decisions for that function.

When targeting functional executives, it is important to select those who are managerially at the proper level to have interest in your background. The rule of thumb is to select those who are organizationally two levels above the position for which you are applying. Such individuals are usually not only aware of specific openings for which you might qualify, but may also be considering the possibility of replacing the individual who might have been your new boss.

By applying at this level, you may increase your chances for employment at more than one level in the organization. Additionally, if your would-be boss is handed your cover letter and resume by his or her boss, along with favorable comments on your candidacy, this may result in a more thorough review of your credentials than might otherwise have been the case. Also, your cover letter and accompanying resume may be just the ticket that convinces the senior manager to approve that employment requisition your would-be boss has been seeking.

As previously stated, whenever possible, you should avoid sending your cover letter to the company's Personnel or Employment functions, since they are often aware only of current openings and may be totally unaware of the line executive's future staffing requirements. Additionally, because he or she may lack specific knowledge of your functional specialty, the Personnel or Employment Manager may not be fully qualified to judge the value of your specialized or technical credentials.

In all cases, it is strongly recommended that you address your cover letter to a specific individual rather than to a functional area. To do otherwise is to further increase the impersonal nature of an already somewhat impersonal correspondence. This will surely cause your star to fall considerably in the eyes of the employer. It suggests that you do not have the resourcefulness or motivation to do the minimal research usually required to uncover this information.

Although the volume of the direct mail campaign will not permit the design of a tailored, personalized introductory paragraph in your cover letter, nonetheless, you should try to make it as interesting as possible in an effort to stimulate readership. The sample cover letters at the end of this chapter should give you some ideas in this regard. Where possible, try to create some curiosity about your qualifications and ability to contribute to the hiring company. Additionally, adopt a businesslike tone and state your interest in employment with the firm.

As the samples will show, your letter should also contain a brief summary of your overall credentials. Normally, this includes the following:

1. Job-relevant degree and major.
2. Number of years of job-related functional experience.
3. Some statement implying your success in this function.

If your academic major is unrelated to the position for which you are applying, a simple statement of degree level (excluding major) will be sufficient. In fact, in such cases, mention of the major may be to your detriment, suggesting to some employers that you don't have the necessary formal education to support your job objective.

Additionally, if you include a statement of your years of experience, be sure not to overdo it. If you are moving into the twilight years of your career, highlighting your 30 or 40 years of experience may be just what the employer needs to practice age discrimination and screen you out before you can even get started. Likewise, if your years of experience seem unusually heavy for the level of the position for which you are applying, this may raise some unnecessary red flags. In such cases, simply state that you have "excellent experience" in the field, excluding any reference to the number of years.

In reviewing the sample general broadcast cover letters found at the end of this chapter, you will also discover that another common element they share is the statement of job-relevant accomplishments, presented in either linear or paragraph form. Since this topic has been discussed in detail earlier in this chapter, we will not belabor the point here. Suffice it to say that the statement of job-relevant accomplishments is an essential element of the cover letter, which serves to market your value-adding capabilities to the prospective employer. This element is key to the effectiveness of your cover letter and should therefore be considered an integral part of your design.

Most well-designed cover letters will include an action-motivating statement of some sort in the last or second-to-last paragraph. This statement either requests action on the part of the employer or states that the author intends to take further action as a follow-up to the correspondence. The sample cover letters illustrate several techniques for accomplishing this. In each case, the action-motivating statement is intended to motivate the employer to contact the applicant or to prepare the employer for future contact by the author. In either case, it is used to keep the relationship moving toward the letter's objective—a job interview.

The final common element of an effective general broadcast cover letter is a statement of appreciation. This is an act of common courtesy and reflects favorably on your good manners and consideration of others. Simply put, this statement thanks the reader for the time that he or she has invested in reviewing your employment credentials. Such sensitivity to the reader's time will usually reflect well on your candidacy.

The remainder of this chapter contains sample general broadcast cover letters for your perusal. You should find them helpful for designing your own broadcast letter.

SAMPLE A   *General Broadcast Letter*

200 East Lansing Street
Benton Harbor, MI 14385
February 22, 1999

Ms. Beatrice A. Fleming
Marketing Director
Saxon Foods, Inc.
10 Saxon Place
Detroit, MI 12739

Dear Ms. Fleming:

Please accept my application for Brand Manager, a position for which I have proven qualifications. Upon review of the enclosed resume, I believe you will be convinced of my ability to contribute almost immediately to Saxon Foods' marketing efforts.

I have enjoyed outstanding success at pumping new life into tired old brands, making them hum. This includes:

- Increased *Frozen Edibles* market share by 80% in only two years.
- Doubled *Tummy Tempters* share of market in just nine months.
- Used targeted direct mail couponing to increase sale of *Little Italy* pizza brand by 25% in 16 months.

My contributions to new brands are equally successful. Please consider the following results:

- Achieved 20% market share penetration for *Magic Meal* within one year of introduction.
- Completed national roll-out of *Tasty Fries* in eight months (achieving 12% of market).

My credentials include an M.B.A. in Marketing from the Harvard Business School, plus ten years of successful major brand experience in both Marketing and Market Research.

Should you have room in your organization for a proven Brand Manager who can have immediate impact on your marketing objectives and contribute significantly to your bottom line, I can be reached at (414) 668-9475. Please leave a voice message, and I will respond promptly.

Thank you for your consideration.

Sincerely,

Samuel B. Bergstrom
Samuel B. Bergstrom

sbb

Enclosure

SAMPLE B   *General Broadcast Letter*

118 Roberts Hall
Bucknell University
Lewisberg, PA 19364
January 3, 1999

Mr. Willard P. Johnson
Director, Marketing and Sales
The Clawson Company, Inc.
201 Independence Square
Philadelphia, PA 19385

Dear Mr. Johnson:

Please accept my resume in application for the position of Salesperson Trainee. I believe I possess the qualities you seek, and would appreciate the opportunity to demonstrate this through a personal interview with your recruiter during your forthcoming interview trip to Bucknell University.

Although short on sales experience, I am long on interest and enthusiasm! My outgoing, friendly nature is ideal for developing and building solid relationships with customers. My bias for action and strong service orientation suggests that I would be immediately responsive to customer needs. My drive, determination and penchant for leadership are, I believe, well evidenced by the following achievements:

- Grade Point Average of 3.6/4.0

- Fraternity President - Senior Year
  Fraternity Vice President - Junior Year
  Fraternity Pledge Chairperson - Sophomore Year

- Varsity Crew Captain - Senior Year
  Varsity Crew Co-Captain - Junior Year
  Varsity Tennis - 4 Years

- Fraternity Play Producer/Director - Senior Year

May I have the opportunity to meet with your company to explore my qualifications for becoming a valuable member of your sales and marketing team?

I will call your office on Wednesday, January 9th to determine your interest and to arrange a suitable time for meeting with your recruiter. Thank you for your consideration.

Sincerely,

Phillip C. Jones
Student

pcj

Enclosure

SAMPLE C   *General Broadcast Letter*

12 Oyster Creek Road
Ocean Meadows, NJ 17384
July 15, 1998

Mr. Frank C. Reardon
President
Flex-Tube, Inc.
12 Industry Row
Princeton, NJ 17284

Dear Mr. Reardon:

As the senior officer of a leading tubing manufacturer, I am sure you can appreciate the difference a strong manufacturing executive can make to a company's bottom line. May I invite you to consider my credentials?

A senior manufacturing executive with an M.B.A. and undergraduate degree in engineering, I have logged nearly fifteen years of highly successful experience and contribution. My record includes:

- 32% manufacturing cost reduction for major furnace operation ($10 million annual savings)
- on-time, below-cost start-up of $550 million tube operation ($19 million savings)
- 84% scrap reduction through TQM effort, saving $5 million annually
- 25% ($6 million) annual labor savings through major reengineering initiative
- 30% raw material cost savings through JIT inventory control ($3 million annually)
- consolidation of 4 plants into 2 with simultaneous productivity increase of 10%

Should we be meeting to explore the contributions I can make to Flex-Tube, Inc. in a senior operations management capacity?

If so, I can be confidentially reached at (609) 739-8475 during working hours, or (609) 344-9762 during the evening.

Thank you for your consideration.

Sincerely yours,

Marshall B. Lewis

Marshall B. Lewis

mbl

Enclosure

SAMPLE D   *General Broadcast Letter*

605 Thorton Lane
Cedarville, MN 18264
June 30, 1997

Ms. Victoria F. Framington
Vice President, Technology
Seabright Chemical Company
200 Shell Lane
Sea Pointe, NJ 18275

Dear Ms. Framington:

As an industry leader in polymer chemistry, Seabright Chemical might be interested in the contributions that could be made by a seasoned polymer scientist with a demonstrated record of success in new product innovation. A Ph.D. in Polymer Chemistry, I have nearly 15 years of proven achievement in the development of new and profitable product lines.

My penchant for creativity is well documented through the award of over 26 registered patents and 22 new product introductions. My efforts have led to more than $100 million annually in new sales contributions. Perhaps I can make similar contributions to Seabright's marketing efforts.

My areas of technical expertise encompass the following chemical specialties:

Organic & Polymer Specialty Chemicals:
- Water Treatment Chemicals
- Oil Field & Mining Chemicals
- Consumer Products (Based on Water Soluble Polymers)

Polymers, Rubbers & Plastics:
- New Polymers & Plastics (Synthetic Approach)
- New Polymers & Plastics (Physio-Chemical Approach)

My current annual income is $95,000, and I have no geographical limitations or restrictions.

Should you have a suitable opening on your technical staff, I would enjoy the opportunity of mutually exploring the contributions I could make to your product development efforts. I can be reached at (603) 439-2974 during business hours (discretion please).

Thank you for your consideration, and I look forward to hearing from you.

Sincerely,

Michael D. Harrison Ph.D.

Michael D. Harrison, Ph.D.

mdh

Enclosure

SAMPLE E   *General Broadcast Letter*

105 Sandy Hook Road
Newport Beach, CA 18375
September 18, 1999

Mr. Craig L. Portsmith
Vice President of Engineering
Kramer Industries, Inc.
305 East River Road
Green Bay, WI 12847

Dear Mr. Portsmith:

I am interested in employment as a Senior Project Engineer with Kramer Industries, Inc. Review of the enclosed resume will reveal that I have strong project experience with Hilton Paper Company, one of your key competitors.

A degreed mechanical engineer with more than 12 years paper machine project engineering experience, I have earned a solid reputation for consistently completing projects on time and under budget. Some major accomplishments include:

- On-time, under-budget $80 million rebuild of paper machine twin-wire former ($6 million savings)

- Lead engineer on design/installation of $150 million Beloit paper machine ($10 million savings - delivered 2 months ahead of schedule)

- Senior project engineer on $40 million paper machine after-dryer rebuild ($1.5 million savings - completed 1 month ahead of schedule)

Although experienced with most machine configurations, I am particularly familiar with twin-wire formation, transpiration drying, and other state-of-the-art sheet formation technology. This should be of particular value to companies seeking to upgrade their papermaking knowledge and capability.

Current compensation is $85,000.

Should you be in the market for someone with strong paper machine project engineering leadership, I would be pleased to hear from you. I can be reached at (714) 693-7042. Thank you.

Sincerely yours,

Scott M. Beatty

Scott Michael Beatty

smb

Enclosure

SAMPLE F   *General Broadcast Letter*

915 Coral Drive
Key West, FL 34948
June 30, 1998

Ms. Cora B. Radcliffe
Vice President of Human Resources
The Barkley Company
20 Mississippi Overview
Memphis, TN 17364

Dear Ms. Radcliffe:

Please accept the enclosed resume as my application for the position of Director of Staffing of The Barkley Company. Should you have an appropriate opportunity, I think you will find my credentials interesting.

I hold an M.S. in Industrial Relations from Michigan State University, and have nearly nine years experience in the Staffing function. This includes six years as Manager of Administrative Staffing for Wilson Enterprises, and over three years as Practice Director for Russell J. Reynolds, arguably the premiere international firm in the Executive Search Industry.

I have managed a Fortune 200 employment function and established an excellent track record in the successful recruitment of highly-productive contributors at the executive, managerial and professional levels. I enjoy a solid reputation for delivering cost-effective, timely and highest-quality employment results. I am skilled in behavioral interview design, and have implemented interviewing and selection training strategies that have substantially improved the organization's ability to consistently hire high-performing personnel at all levels.

If you are seeking a knowledgeable leader who can upgrade your staffing results, may I suggest we arrange a meeting to explore employment possibilities with your company.

Thank you for your consideration.

Sincerely.

Brice W. Dalton

Brice W. Dalton

bwd

Enclosure

SAMPLE G   *General Broadcast Letter*

95 Breakers View
Newport, RI 17264
April 6, 1998

Mr. Hans B. Haeuser
Manager of Corporate Accounting
Armstrong World Industries, Inc.
Armstrong Plaza
Lancaster, PA 12847

Dear Mr. Haeuser:

I have enclosed my resume to facilitate your consideration of my employment candidacy for the position of Cost Accountant in Armstrong's Corporate Accounting function. I believe I have excellent credentials for this position, and would welcome your interest in my candidacy.

An accounting graduate of Boston College with over five years of professional experience, I have a solid foundation in both auditing and cost accounting. Following two years as an Auditor with Price Waterhouse, I spent nearly three years in manufacturing cost accounting with Reddington Corporation, a $300 million manufacturer of specialty fasteners for the aircraft and aerospace industries. I am now seeking an opportunity to perform manufacturing cost analysis at the macro rather than plant level.

In my current position, I have assumed a leadership role in the identification of significant cost savings opportunities. Through my cost analysis, I have led cross-functional cost reduction efforts that have saved more than $5 million in the last year alone. Other initiatives, now under way, are targeted to deliver another $8 to $10 million cost savings over the next two to three years.

My personal performance ratings have been consistently at the highest level, and I can furnish excellent references who will substantiate my contributions to Reddington.

May I have the opportunity to explore career opportunities at Armstrong? If so, I can be reached at (623) 992-2738. I look forward to the possibility of meeting with you.

Thank you for considering my employment candidacy.

Sincerely,

Barbara A. Winners

Barbara A. Winners

baw

Enclosure

SAMPLE H   *General Broadcast Letter*

1425 Gaynor Road
Austin, TX 12847
October 22, 1997

Ms. Linda C. McIntyre
Chief Financial Officer
Franklin Technologies, Inc.
1215 Technology Way
Royal Oaks, TX 18236

Dear Ms. McIntyre:

Are you in the market for a skilled Financial Analyst with a successful track record in the identification and analysis of profitable acquisition candidates? If so, I may be the person you are seeking.

A Wharton School M.B.A. with over six years acquisition analysis experience with a premiere, Fortune 100 consumer products company, I have identified and provided comprehensive financial analysis of over 25 acquisition candidates in eight different industries. Candidates have ranged in size from $6 million to over $8 billion in annual revenues. Industries have run the gamut from toy manufacturers, to consulting services, to computer chip manufacturers.

A sampling of results includes:

- acquisition of a $30 million baking company with 22% average ROI in first two years

- $55 million plastic wrap manufacturing acquisition yielding 18% ROI in first year

- acquisition of a $22 million food distribution company with third year ROI of 14%

All companies acquired through my evaluation and recommendation have been profitable, with the lowest annual ROI standing at 6.2%. Additionally, all acquisition targets were successfully acquired at an average price of 1.6 times net profit. I played a key role in formulating negotiation strategy.

I would welcome the opportunity to discuss how I could be of assistance to Franklin Technologies in meeting their growth objectives through successful acquisition of profitable growth companies. Should you wish to explore this possibility, I can be reached in the evening at (713) 974-1906.

Thank you.

Sincerely,

Marguerite E. Ballantine

Marguerite E. Ballantine

meb

Enclosure

SAMPLE I   *General Broadcast Letter*

135 Washington Highway
Scottsdale, AZ 14375
December 22, 1999

Mr. George D. McFarland
Vice President, Logistics
North American Industries, Inc.
825 North Wacker Drive
Chicago, IL 93228

Dear Mr. McFarland:

As the senior Logistics executive of a major corporation, you may be in need of an energetic and results-oriented Procurement Manager who can deliver immediate profits to your bottom line.

The high-performing Senior Purchasing Agent for a $1.2 billion, Fortune 300 food processing and distribution company, I enjoy a reputation for being a tough but fair negotiator who has made significant cost-savings contributions to my employer. Results have included:

- realized $46 million annual savings through implementation of raw materials JIT program
- contributed $32 million annual savings through centralized packaging contract purchases
- saved $18 million annually through conversion to bio-mass fuels and long-term contracts
- sold excess bio-mass energy back to utility company generating $5 million annual revenue
- negotiated three-year office supplies contract worth $2 million savings annually

Further, I pioneered and led a major procurement reengineering project allowing manager direct purchases of less than $1,000 through use of a corporate American Express Card, thus eliminating the need for purchase order processing for nearly 80% of all transactions. This highly innovative approach will allow a 40% reduction in Procurement staff, with estimated annual savings of $20 million.

My credentials include an M.B.A. in Finance from the University of Michigan and an undergraduate degree in Packaging Engineering from Michigan State. Current compensation is $85,000.

Should you feel I could contribute to your organization, I can be reached at (912) 366-9837.

Thank you.

Sincerely,

Karen B. Robinson

Karen B. Robinson

kbr

Enclosure

SAMPLE J   *General Broadcast Letter*

1632 La Dolsa Drive
Reno, NV 13249
May 14, 1998

Ms. Katherine A. Jamieson
Director of Logistics
Byzantine Corporation
12 Commerce Drive
Key Largo, FL 18374

Dear Ms. Jamieson:

I am interested in employment as a Procurement Manager with Byzantine Corporation. As a leading consumer products company, I felt that you may have a need for a procurement professional with strong reengineering skills and extensive experience in the large-scale purchase of flexible packaging and corrugated supplies.

My procurement experience encompasses over 15 years with a Fortune 200 consumer products company, where I managed an annual packaging materials budget of over $250 million. Specific accomplishments include:

- Negotiated 20% reduction in corporate knock-down costs through long-term contract ($20 million annual savings).

- Implemented JIT contract for shrink wrap purchases saving $15 million annually.

- Pioneered "shared purchases" concept, uniting corrugated purchases of 4 companies resulting in $12 million annual cost savings.

- Led reengineering study of vital supply purchasing, identifying over $80 million potential annual savings through implementation of revolutionary procurement concepts.

Should you feel that I could contribute added value to your organization, I would appreciate if you would call me at (306) 374-9738. I would welcome the opportunity to discuss career prospects with your organization.

Thank you for your consideration, and I look forward to your reply.

Sincerely,

Christopher T. Beatty

Christopher Todd Beatty

ctb

Enclosure

SAMPLE K   *General Broadcast Letter*

216 Wilson Drive
Framingham, CT 13295
October 15, 2005

Ms. Barbara. A. Haffer
Chief Information Officer
Mannington Corporation
400 Technology Row
Cleveland, OH 12958

Dear Ms. Haffer:

Could you be on the lookout for a motivated, accomplished Information Technology Project Manager with a reputation for innovation and a penchant for cost savings through effective systems selection and implementation? If so, I think you might find my qualifications intriguing.

Here is a brief sampling of successful projects I have led, and contributions I have made to my last two employers:

- Designed and implemented an international communications network that doubled traffic capacity for all data, image, and voice traffic between North America, Europe, and Asia while simultaneously reducing costs by 15%.

- Selected and implemented new accounting software system that reduced accounting staff by 25% and compressed closing cycles by four workdays.

- Created a central data network and desktop support team providing expanded services while reducing labor costs by 33%.

- Reduced business process cycle times by 20% through implementation on LAN- and WAN-based information sharing applications.

My credentials include an M.B.A. from Columbia University coupled with an M.S. in Computer Science from Ohio State.

I am most interested in talking with you about career opportunities at Mannington, and would welcome a call from you. I can be reached at (603) 347-8374 during the day or via email at TFM22@ATT.net.

Thank you for your consideration.

Sincerely,

Terrance F. Masters

Terrance F. Masters

tfm

Enclosure

SAMPLE L   *General Broadcast Letter*

822 Green Lane
Kansas City, KS 18328
August 25, 2004

Mr. Barton S. Giles
Vice President of Public Affairs
Tycor Foods, Inc.
655 Industry Way
Dallas, TX 25385

Dear Mr. Giles:

Enclosed please find my resume for your consideration.

I seek a corporate position in public affairs and/or communications with a growth-oriented company offering career advancement for a top communications professional who has the ability to meaningfully impact bottom-line results. I am such a professional!

Please consider some recent contributions at Berry Cola Company:

- Created and published a 100-page award-winning book, *Berry Cola Recipes*, which received favorable reviews in newspapers across the country and was ordered by over 2 million consumers.
- Directed development of a strategy to boost the company's visibility and support among Hispanics, generating strong national media coverage and ongoing ties to Hispanic leaders.
- Recommended, booked, and produced national entertainment acts, employing well-known celebrities, which generated substantial media coverage and greatly raised awareness and interest in Berry Cola among the consuming public.
- Prepared numerous press releases attracting attention of key industry analysts and creating image of Berry Cola as an emerging industry leader and favored stock pick.

My credentials include an M.B.A. from the University of Chicago, with emphasis in Communications, and an undergraduate degree in Communications from Rutgers University, where I was a Barkley Communications Fellow and a Cum Laude graduate.

Should you be interested in learning more, please contact me at (712) 553-2257 during evening hours or send an email to my personal email address at LinCal@AOL.com.

Thank you for your time and consideration.

Sincerely,

Linda B. Calvert

Linda B. Calvert

lbc

Enclosure

SAMPLE M   *General Broadcast Letter*

509 Sperry Way
Pensacola, FL 21840
February 2, 2005

Mr. Nathan F. Barrington
President & CEO
American Metal Specialties, Inc.
62 Commerce Way, SW
Atlanta, GA 12238

Dear Mr. Barrington:

I am an accomplished attorney with a law degree from Yale University and over 20 years experience in the metals industry, including the last 5 years as Vice President and General Counsel of Sterling Silver Corporation. I have enclosed my resume for your reference.

Some key accomplishments that may be of particular interest to you include:

- Crafted a program, acceptable to the EPA, for cleanup of ninety years of mining waste while avoiding "Superfund" designation, thus saving millions of dollars in oversight costs.

- Successfully negotiated $800 million acquisition of Fargo, Inc., a mining, oil & gas, and heavy metals company, at highly favorable terms.

- Negotiated and oversaw drafting of all engineering and construction contracts for $520 million smelter construction project, saving considerable outside legal fees.

- Supervised antitrust, securities, product liability, toxic tort, real estate, and trademark litigation for Bethlehem Steel Corporation with notable results.

My strong negotiation and litigation skills, coupled with specific metal industry experience, uniquely qualify me for the position of General Council of a firm such as yours. I would welcome the opportunity to discuss the many contributions I could make to the bottom line of American Metal Specialties.

Should you have an interest in my qualifications, please call me at (312) 663-9021. Since Sterling is unaware of this inquiry, please treat this matter in strictest confidence.

Thank you for your consideration.

Sincerely,

Michael R. Dresher

Michael R. Dresher

mrd

Enclosure

SAMPLE N   *General Broadcast Letter*

1835 South Beach Road
Oceanside, CA 23445
March 16, 2006

Ms. Katherine Steinman
Director of Corporate Packaging
Beaumont Cosmetic Company, Inc.
1225 McArthur Blvd.
Irvine, CA 43289

Dear Ms. Steinman:

As a Senior Packaging Engineer in the Cosmetic Industry, I have long admired the creative packaging work of Beaumont Cosmetics Company. I enjoy a reputation for being unusually creative as well, and this has ignited a natural attraction to your company. Please, therefore, consider my credentials for a position as a member of your corporate packaging development team.

Examples of my creativity include:

- Developed all packaging concepts for Loral Cosmetic's *Breathless* brand of women's perfumes, resulting in one of the company's most successful product launches in its entire history.

- Developed unique pump dispenser for *He Man After Shave*, resulting in 4 U.S. patents and propelling product to #4 in its brand category within 3 years from market entry.

- Developed revolutionary commercial hand lotion dispenser, allowing product to be pumped to as many as 12 counter dispensers from a single large volume reservoir. (2 U.S. patents)

- Partnered with major aerosol vendor to create universal package design that is environmentally and legally acceptable worldwide, reducing corporate-wide packaging inventory by 30% and saving $3.5 million annually.

My background includes an M.S. in Packaging Engineering from Michigan State University and over 12 years packaging design and development in the cosmetic field.

I would welcome the opportunity to explore how my creative talents and packaging engineering skills could be effectively used to further enhance the fine reputation of Beaumont Cosmetic's Packaging Department as a top packaging leader in the cosmetics field.

I can be reached at (914) 332-9837 or via email at CalMar@MSN.net.

Thank you for your consideration.

Sincerely,

Calvin B. Marshall

Calvin B. Marshall

Enclosure

8

EXECUTIVE SEARCH
COVER LETTERS

The cover letter used to transmit your resume to an executive search firm, although a type of broadcast letter, differs from the general broadcast letter used to correspond with employers. This difference has to do with the needs of these two organizations. Let's examine these needs.

The employer's motivation when reading a cover letter and attached resume is to hire someone who will add value to the corporation. In this regard, he or she is looking for evidence that the candidate has the ability to solve certain key problems, apply new methods and technology, and generally assist in the attainment of the organization's strategic goals and mission.

If the employer has done the necessary homework, the basic knowledge, skills, and capabilities needed to successfully perform the key functions of the job have been identified. The employer then translates these factors into selection criteria against which prospective candidates will be measured.

Additionally, if proper care is taken to select persons who will be both successful and happy in the organization, the employer must also attempt to determine how compatible job candidates will be with the culture of the organization. To do this properly, the employer must define certain personal traits and characteristics, philosophy, and style that will best fit the organization's culture. These factors are added to the list of previously determined technical qualifications to arrive at candidate selection criteria.

When formulating selection criteria, forward-thinking companies also consider another dimension, which has to do with the strategic changes that the organization will need to make if it is to be successful in realizing its longer-term strategic objectives. The employer then translates these changes into new knowledge and skill requirements necessary to drive the required changes needed to realize corporate goals.

The final result of this in-depth analysis of the current job, organizational culture, and the organization's strategic needs is a list of specific selection criteria against which employment candidates will be measured during the interview and employment selection process.

Although an executive search firm may participate to some degree in defining these selection criteria, most of them have already been fairly well-defined by the employer prior to the search firm's arrival on the scene. Thus the executive search firm does not normally have the same level of in-depth understanding of the hiring organization's requirements. Instead, in most cases, the search consultant simply discusses the selection criteria with the employer to make sure they are understood, and then sets off to find the candidate who best meets them.

In short, the employer is looking for someone who will be value adding, while the search firm is looking for someone who best matches the selection criteria. The search firm therefore typically has a more narrow perspective than does the employer, who has the benefit of knowing all of the various intricacies and special internal needs of his or her organization thereby reading the cover letter in search of evidence that the candidate will be value adding. The search firm, on the other hand, typically views the cover letter as a simple letter of transmittal, and moves quickly to the resume to make a comparison between the candidate's qualifications and the selection criteria.

The cover letter is far less likely to make a sale to the executive search firm than it is to the employer. This fact suggests, then, that the cover letters used to transmit your resume to these two organizations need to be handled differently.

Letter Elements

The basic elements of the executive search cover letter are as follows:

1. Return address.
2. Date.
3. Search firm address.
4. Salutation.
5. Introductory paragraph or statement.
6. Statement of job objective.
7. Brief summary of qualifications.
8. Value-adding statement (optional).
9. Reason for making change (optional).
10. Salary requirements (optional).
11. Geographical preferences/restrictions (optional).
12. Statement of willingness to provide additional information.
13. Instructions for reaching you.

14. Statement of appreciation.
15. Complimentary close.
16. Signature.

Introductory Paragraph

The introductory paragraph usually accomplishes two things. First, it acknowledges the role of the executive search firm in helping client organizations find key professionals and executives. Second, it states your job objective.

Here are some typical introductory paragraphs:

I am currently seeking a senior-level position in manufacturing management. Perhaps one of your current search assignments requires such an individual.

I am a seasoned financial executive with Fortune 100 experience. Please consider the enclosed resume in light of your current assignments for top financial management talent.

I have decided to make a career change and am currently seeking a position as a CEO or COO. Please consider my background for any appropriate active or future executive search assignments requiring someone with my credentials.

As you can see, the statement of job objective is usually included in the opening paragraph along with the request to be considered as a candidate for current or future assignments.

Read the sample cover letters at the end of this chapter for some additional ideas on how to structure your lead-in paragraph.

Qualifications Summary

The executive search cover letter normally contains a paragraph that briefly summarizes the candidate's overall qualifications. This includes educational credentials as well as professional work experience.

When summarizing work experience, it is important to cite only what is supportive of your stated job objective. Don't bore the reader by including nonrelated assignments. Also, be brief. Stick to only the basic information needed to crystalize your qualifications, and don't drone on and on with the details of your background. If well-written, your resume will accomplish all of this.

The following are some sample qualification summaries. Additional examples are found at the end of this chapter.

I hold an M.B.A. in Marketing from the University of Chicago and a B.S. in Mechanical Engineering from the University of Michigan. My background includes nearly eighteen years in marketing and sales management, with the last five years as Director of Marketing for the Cranston Corporation, a Fortune 200 manufacturer of fastening devices.

A graduate of the University of Delaware with an M.S. in Chemical Engineering, I have been employed in the Central Research Group of the DuPont Company for the last nine years, where I have become thoroughly versed in synthetic fiber development. My creativity as a Research Scientist is supported by eight current patents with an additional six pending.

I am a seasoned project engineer with over twelve years experience in paper machine project engineering. I have successfully managed paper machine capital projects valued at over $80 million. My professional credentials include an M.S. in Mechanical Engineering and a Professional Engineer license from the Commonwealth of Pennsylvania.

Value-Adding Statement (Optional)

A value-adding statement is intended to convey your ability to make meaningful contributions to the search firm's client organization. As indicated, although important to the general broadcast cover letter, it is considered optional in the executive search cover letter. If cleverly written, this statement can have a positive impact on the reader, but for the most part, it is considered to have little impact on the decision of the executive search firm, where the focus is on matching qualifications with the client organization's requirements, not on value adding. The search firm's main focus is thus on the resume rather than on the cover letter that introduces it.

The value-adding statement(s) usually consists of major job-related accomplishments. These are carefully tailored to the anticipated needs of the employer and normally fall into one or more of the following categories:

1. Related to the ongoing functional objectives of the job.
2. Related to the strategic goals of the hiring organization.
3. The ability to apply new methods and state-of-the-art technology.

The following are some examples of value-adding statements for your review. Certain of the sample cover letters at the end of this chapter also contain such statements.

The following key accomplishments as a manufacturing executive should provide evidence of my ability to make meaningful contributions to one of your client organizations:

- *Reengineered manufacturing organization resulting in 20% headcount reduction and annual savings of $3 million.*
- *Installed Deming-based total quality program accounting for 22% scrap reduction ($1.2 million annual savings) and 80% reduction in customer complaints.*
- *Instituted JIT methods for control of raw materials inventory—$1 million annual savings.*

As a seasoned project engineering manager, I can make significant contributions to one of your clients. Consider the following achievements:

- *Successfully managed $20 million capital expansion of Templeton Mill—completed on time and 10% under budget.*
- *Installed TDC 2000 control system in the converting department of Wilmington Plant—annual savings of $2 million.*
- *Developed, designed, and installed new web forming device, increasing machine speeds by 18%—annual savings of $1.7 million.*

My resume will attest that, as an internal Organization Effectiveness Consultant, I have consistently provided state-of-the-art leadership in applying the most recent thinking to major program development. Perhaps I can make similar contributions to one of your clients. Please consider the following accomplishments:

- *Transitioned major manufacturing organization from traditional departmental structure to customer-focused, product stream organization.*
- *Worked with Senior Vice President to successfully transition key division from traditional management philosophy to a participatory management-based system.*

- *Trained over 200 middle and senior managers in the use of facilitator skills and management process design concepts.*

In each of the examples, you will note that the author utilizes language that encourages the executive search firm to make the connection between the accomplishments cited and the value that could be derived through your employment by one of the firm's clients.

Reason for Making Change (Optional)

As indicated, providing the search firm with a specific reason for wanting to make a change is optional. From an initial screening standpoint, it seldom adds to cover letter effectiveness and may, in fact, be detrimental to your employment campaign depending upon circumstances.

This subject was discussed in detail in Chapter 6, "Cover Letter Inclusions/Exclusions." Review Chapter 6 for the guidelines. For the most part, however, explaining your reasons for change is unnecessary and adds little to the effectiveness of the executive search cover letter.

Salary Requirements (Optional)

Generally, the inclusion of salary requirements is considered optional in the executive search cover letter. It is usually to your benefit, however, to exclude such information. In this way, you assure yourself of maximum flexibility and control by not automatically screening yourself from consideration on the basis of income requirements that are considered too high for a given opportunity. Nevertheless, there are times when you may want to include your compensation requirements in the letter. This is particularly true when you are currently employed and unwilling to consider a lower compensation level, regardless of the opportunity.

If you elect to include your salary requirements in the cover letter, however, remember that there is always the unusual opportunity that, regardless of short-term income reduction, may offer significant future advancement and corresponding income growth potential considerably beyond that of your current position.

Geographical Preferences/Restrictions (Optional)

As with salary requirements, inclusion of a statement concerning geographical preferences or restrictions may be somewhat limiting, and might serve to screen you out from a career opportunity that you might otherwise deem very desirable. Why take this chance?

It is felt that inclusion of geographical factors does little to enhance the overall effectiveness of executive search cover letters and, in most cases, can actually prove detrimental. Remember, if the executive search firm approaches you about a particular opportunity with one of its clients, you can always decline the chance to pursue it should geographical factors not be to your liking.

By being open to geographical considerations, you at least allow yourself the chance to weigh this factor against other, perhaps more important criteria, such as future growth and potential. If the opportunity for advancement is unusually good, you may just decide to waive geographical considerations. By excluding them from the cover letter, you at least preserve your options rather than prematurely foreclose on what might be an excellent job opportunity. The decision, of course, is up to you.

You may now wish to review the following sample executive search cover letters for some ideas on structuring your own. I hope you will find them helpful.

SAMPLE A   *Executive Search Cover Letter*

108 Baker Lane
Mobile, AL 16354
January 16, 1998

Mr. Orson B. Smathers
Senior Partner
Smathers & Cooper
25 Wacker Drive
Chicago, IL 13285

Dear Mr. Smathers:

Could one of your Chicago-based or national clients use a successful and experienced engineering executive or program director to head up a major effort?

My broad manufacturing, engineering, and development background in the computer equipment and office automation industries, coupled with an excellent track record of new product introductions, may well be of interest to one of your client companies.

My credentials include an M.S. in Electrical Engineering coupled with over 15 years engineering and electronics product development experience in the computer and related electronics field. This includes over six years as Technology Director for Dynatech, a $300 million manufacturer of computer chips and printed circuit boards. My specific accomplishments are well documented on the enclosed resume.

Although technical and managerial challenges are of highest priority to me, you may wish to be aware that my total compensation has been in the $135,000 range in the last few years.

Should my background be of interest to you, please contact me during the day at (305) 795-2375 or at my home at (305) 688-4275 during evening hours.

Thank you for your consideration.

Sincerely,

Carolyn A. Baker

Carolyn A. Baker

cab

Enclosure

SAMPLE B   *Executive Search Cover Letter*

309 Grant Blvd.
Richmond, VA 12736
September 22, 1998

Ms. Cynthia A. Baxter
Senior Partner
Lane, Baxter and Roe, Inc.
220 Oliver Street, N.E.
Atlanta, GA 13648

Dear Ms. Baxter:

I am seeking career advancement opportunities as a manager or executive in the field of Organization Development. Positions in either manufacturing or consulting would be of interest to me. Perhaps one of your clients may be interested in my candidacy.

As a Ph.D. in Organization Design and Development, my eight years of corporate-level assignments have encompassed the full range of Organization and Management Development activities, advancing from stand-up trainer to strategy development at the corporate management level. More recently, I have been serving as part-time evening faculty in the Organization Development Masters degree program at the University of Richmond. This has been augmented by a variety of Organization Design and Development consulting assigments with local and national companies on a part-time basis during the day.

Although I would prefer to remain in the Richmond area, I would be quite open to the prospects of relocation should the right opportunity present itself.

Should one of your clients have a suitable opportunity, I would appreciate hearing from you. I can be reached at my office on a confidential basis during the day or at my home in the evening. Both phone numbers are included on the enclosed resume.

Thank you.

Sincerely,

Martin D. Trainor

Martin D. Trainor

mdt

Enclosure

SAMPLE C   *Executive Search Cover Letter*

25 East Main Street
Columbus, OH 13948
November 30, 1999

Mr. Cortland B. Darring
Senior Principal
Darring, Smith and Braxton
Executive Search Consultants
20 Ivory Tower Suites
315 Capital Parkway
Washington, DC 18236

Dear Mr. Darring:

My resume is enclosed for your review against the needs of your clients for a Senior Financial Officer or Corporate Controller. In the event that you do not have an active assignment for such a position, I would appreciate if you would retain my file for future reference.

My background includes an M.B.A. in Finance from the Wharton School, coupled with over 15 years of increasing management responsibility in the fields of accounting and finance. I am currently Corporate Controller of Utex Corporation, a $200 million manufacturer of commercial spraying equipment, where I report directly to the President and manage a staff of 32 employees.

Growth prospects at Utex are nonexistent, and I have recently elected to pursue outside career opportunities. My primary interest is in becoming C.F.O. of a medium-sized growth company, however, I would also seriously consider a position as a corporate or division-level Controller for a major company.

My current compensation is in the $130,000 range, however, job challenge and career advancement are primary motivating factors at this point in my career.

If one of your clients is seeking someone with my credential, I would appreciate a call. If necessary, you can reach me at my office at (319) 874-9028. My preference is for evening calls at (319) 699-0407.

Thank you for your consideration.

Sincerely,

Warren A. Littles

Warren A. Littles

wal

Enclosure

SAMPLE D   *Executive Search Cover Letter*

32 West Carlton Lane
St. Louis, MO 13829
August 15, 1998

Ms. Janet B. Longwood
Vice President
Beesley, Kilmer & Schmidt
205 Industry Circle
Houston, TX 71395

Dear Ms. Longwood:

I am seeking a senior-level position in Operations management. Perhaps a current or future client may have an interest in my capabilities.

I hold an M.S. degree in Industrial Management from Ohio State University and have over 16 years experience in Operations, with 8 years in a management capacity. Currently Director of Operations for Baxter Corporation, a $250 million specialty pumps manufacturer, I manage a staff of 25 and direct all manufacturing for a six-plant operation.

In my current position, I have saved nearly $18 million through various innovative programs implemented over the last four years. These have included major initiatives in reengineering, TQM, JIT, MRP, and product stream management. I pride myself in staying current in the latest, state-of-the-art developments in the field of Operations management, and am frequently one of the first to try them. I am firmly committed to the concept of continuous improvement.

If one of your clients is seeking a professional Operations executive, who has established a strong record of cost reduction and productivity improvement, perhaps I may be their candidate. Please keep me in mind as appropriate search assignments develop.

Should you wish to contact me during working hours, I can be reached at (512) 374-0947 on a confidential basis.

Thank you for your consideration.

Sincerely,

B. C. Schwartz

Bernard C. Schwartz

bcs

Enclosure

SAMPLE E   *Executive Search Cover Letter*

12 Conner Road
Portsmouth, NH 12847
June 21, 1998

Mr. Donald S. Kingston
Senior Vice President
Brammer, Simpson & Cramer
Consultants in Executive Search
135 Wilshire Highway
Dallas, TX 13829

Dear Mr. Kingston:

It has come to my attention that your firm specializes in executive search in the Logistics-related fields. I am seeking a senior management position in Procurement, and would welcome your review of my credentials against current search assignments in this field.

The enclosed resume will show that I have an M.B.A. in Industrial Management from the University of New Hampshire and an undergraduate degree in Industrial Engineering from the same school. My professional experience includes over 20 years in Logistics-related areas, including over 10 years in Procurement management.

I have an excellent track record in orchestrating major cost reduction and efficiency improvement in the various Procurement functions I have managed. My forte has been in successfully negotiating major long-term raw materials and vital supplies contracts that have saved millions and helped my employers maintain a competitive edge. Initiation of JIT delivery has substantially reduced in-house inventory investments and freed up nearly $30 million in operating capital for my current employer. Perhaps I could make similar contributions to one of your clients.

My compensation currently stands at $120,000 per year, and I am open to relocation with the exception of the East Coast metropolitan areas.

Should you require further information, I can be reached during business hours, on a confidential basis, at (912) 349-5869.

Thank you.

Sincerely,

Beverly A. Thompson

Beverly A. Thompson

bat

Enclosure

SAMPLE F   *Executive Search Cover Letter*

31 North Grove Street
Cedarville, NC 13486
May 26, 1998

Ms. Connie D. Dennison
Senior Principal
Dennison & Smith, Inc.
233 North Tower Road
Atlanta, GA 13285

Dear Ms. Dennison:

Perhaps one of your current assignments calls for a seasoned Director of Research in specialty
chemicals, who can provide strong leadership to the firm's technology efforts. If so, they may
find my credentials quite interesting.

A Ph.D. in Organic Chemistry from the Georgia Institute of Technology, my background includes
18 years in specialty chemicals research and development, both as a scientist and as a manager.
Currently Director of Research for Wexler Chemicals, a $350 million manufacturer of specialty
chemicals sold to the Pulp & Paper Industry, I report to the President and manage an 80-person
research staff focused on advance research and applications development of paper machine wet-
end chemical specialties.

In the last five years as Wexler's research director, I have led the development and successful
introduction of over 30 new products. These have increased company sales from $110 million to
$350 million and increased profitability by a corresponding 300%. Perhaps I could significantly
boost one of your clients technology efforts as well.

I am open to relocation, but would prefer an East Coast metropolitan area where available.
Annual compensation is in the $115,000 range, and I am looking to significantly improve upon
this with my next move.

Should you have an interest, please contact me during the day at (326) 773-8847.

I appreciate your consideration.

Sincerely,

Barry W. Sanders

Barry W. Sanders

bws

Enclosure

SAMPLE G   *Executive Search Cover Letter*

126 Weymouth Road
Springfield, MA 32816
April 23, 2005

Ms. Carolyn S. Heddeman
Senior Partner
The Heddeman Partners
1442 Liberty Street
Boston, MA 53729

Dear Ms. Heddeman:

According to the *Directory of Executive Recruiters*, The Heddeman Partners specializes in the placement of senior level Human Resources executives. I am therefore submitting my resume for your consideration in connection with senior HR search assignments on which you may be currently working.

I hold an M.S. in Industrial Psychology from the University of Minnesota, and have over 15 years experience in the field of Human Resources, 10 with PepsiCo and the last 5 with Kimberly Clark where I am now Director of Human Resources for the Corporate Staff. I am seeking a position as Vice President of Human Resources for a medium or large-sized consumer products company where I can further expand my scope of responsibility and more fully challenge my executive management skills.

Significant accomplishments include:

- Implemented HRScope™, a competency-based strategic software system that fully integrates HR and business strategy and provides a sound quantitative basis for human capital management.
- Successfully negotiated 3-year labor contract with the United Pulp & Paper Workers, with major concessions in medical insurance and premium pay provisions (annual savings of $4.2 million).
- Key member of acquisition team in the successful acquisitions of Jackson Paper Company and Valley Pulp, Inc., providing initial due diligence and then leading post-acquisition integration.
- Provided corporate leadership as the principal O.D. consultant in the company's shift to a team-based, high-performance culture, resulting in major reorganization and a 25% reduction in staff.

Although open to relocation, I have a slight preference for the Southeastern states. Compensation requirements are in the $150,000 base range plus performance-based incentives.

Should you have an appropriate opportunity, I would welcome a call from you or a member of your staff. It is best to contact me at (610) 322-3857 during evening hours or via email at WilBar@AOL.com.

Thank you.

Sincerely,

Wilbur D. Barlow

Wilbur D. Barlow

Enclosure

SAMPLE H   *Executive Search Cover Letter*

827 North 16th Street
Costa Mesa, CA 13885
July 17, 2006

Mr. Jonathan S. Saunders
Partner
Clearfield & Saunders, LLP
200 College Avenue
Irvine, CA 23847

Dear Mr. Saunders:

My research shows that Clearfield & Saunders, LLP is one of the leading executive search firms in the field of Operations Management. Please, therefore, accept my resume for consideration against the requirements of any appropriate client Operations Management search assignments on which you may currently be working.

I am a successful manufacturing executive with a M.S. in Mechanical Engineering and over 14 years experience in production management, the last 6 of which have been as Plant Manager of Walden Pump's 650-employee Riverside manufacturing facility. I am now seeking a senior level Operations Management position at the corporate or division level, with multi-plant P&L responsibility.

As the enclosed resume will confirm, I have established a strong reputation as a turnaround expert with the ability to quickly convert losing operations to cash positive contributors. I am a skilled participative manager and team builder, who believes in the concept of leadership-by-example. I am credited with converting two downtrodden, low morale plant workforces into highly energized, motivated, and productive organizations that now take great pride in the quality and efficiency of their work.

If one of your clients is seeking a skilled and seasoned operations executive with a strong track record as a motivational leader and bottom-line contributor, I would welcome a call from you.

I can be reached, on a confidential basis, at (301) 775-3957 or by email at MarKen@MSN.net.

Thank you, and I look forward to hearing from you.

Sincerely,

Martin F. Kennedy

Martin F. Kennedy

Enclosure

SAMPLE I   *Executive Search Cover Letter*

215 Prince Avenue
West Reading, PA 19348
April 22, 2004

The Kirkland Group
816 Chestnut Street
Philadelphia, PA 19113

Dear Sir/Madam:

I am an experienced Accounting executive seeking a new opportunity to advance my career in the fields of Accounting or Financial Management. Several of my accomplishments have been highlighted on the enclosed resume.

My technical credentials, along with the ability to successfully manage rapid growth and develop subordinates, are well documented and should allow me to make significant contributions to the right company.

I have no geographical restrictions, and compensation requirements are in the mid $100 K range. Compensation is negotiable as appropriate with the specific opportunity.

Since my employer is unaware of my decision to seek other employment, please treat this inquiry with appropriate sensitivity. I can be reached discreetly at work, (610) 442-9987, or via email at MarStan@ATT.net.

Thank you for your consideration.

Sincerely,

Margaret A. Stantford

Margaret A. Stantford

Enclosure

SAMPLE J   *Executive Search Cover Letter*

River Walk Apartments, # 26A
235 Front Street
St. Louis, MO 21385
June 16, 2005

The Kennett Group
Executive Search Consultants
1625 Wacker Drive
Chicago, IL 31286

Dear Sir/Madam:

As a leading search firm in the field of Sales Management, you may have an interest in my credentials. Please consider my qualifications for appropriate search assignments in sales management at either the regional or national level.

As the enclosed resume shows, I hold a B.A. degree in Marketing from Ohio State University and have over 10 years sales management experience in the consumer products industry. During the last 4 years, I have been Midwest Regional Manager for Procter & Gamble in the sale of its Charmin paper products line to large retail chain stores and consumer discount buyers' clubs.

Some key accomplishments include:

- Increased regional sales volume by 28% in the last 2 years, despite poor economy.
- Propelled Charmin to the # 1 supplier in 3 key national accounts (Wal-Mart, Target, and Krogers).
- Instrumental in the development and coaching of the company's top 2 District Sales Managers (both since promoted to Regional Manager).

I am a highly motivated sales executive with strong reputation for consistent development of superior performers. Compensation requirements are in the $160 K range, and I am geographically flexible.

I look forward to hearing from you, should you feel you have a suitable opportunity appropriate to my qualifications.

Thank you for your consideration.

Sincerely,

David R. Crosby

David R. Crosby

Enclosure

9

ADVERTISING RESPONSE COVER LETTERS

Employment advertising, whether in the local newspaper or in a specialty publication, has long been an important resource for experienced employment professionals seeking to fill positions within their companies. This does not mean that, although frequently used, such advertising is particularly effective. In fact, knowledgeable employment sources estimate that only between 10 and 14 percent of all jobs filled in the United States are filled as a result of advertising. This compares with an estimated 70 percent filled through personal contact and employment networking. Nonetheless, advertisements are considered an important source in job hunting and should therefore be a part of your job search campaign.

It is important to be aware that employment advertising can be found in a wide variety of publications. The most common is the classified section of the newspaper. There are, however, several other publications that should be regularly checked for job opportunities. These include specialty newspapers (i.e., *The National Business Employment Weekly* and *The National Ad Search*), professional association newsletters, trade association publications, and specialty publications related to specific professions and industries (i.e., trade journals and periodicals) which are appropriate to your background and experience.

Employers long ago learned that specialty publications can be a particularly productive source for employment advertising. This is because they are targeted toward a very specific audience. For example, when searching for technical professionals, many employers in the pulp and paper industry will frequently advertise in the *Tappi Journal*, a monthly periodical published by the Technical Association of the Pulp and Paper Industry and mailed to thousands of industry technical and manufacturing professionals. Similar specialized publications exist for many professions and industries. A little research at your local library will help you to identify them. A call to your professional or industry association can also prove helpful in acquiring this information.

Some Differences

The cover letter used to respond to employment advertising is different from the general broadcast letter sent to employers or executive search firms. In particular, it is more targeted and focused, and is specifically directed to the requirements of the employer as set forth in the advertisement.

Actually, employment candidates have a decided advantage when designing a cover letter that responds to recruitment advertising. Unlike the general mailing campaign, where the candidate must do considerable industry research to define the employer's probable needs, the advertisement usually spells out these requirements in specific detail. This allows the applicant to design a highly targeted response that focuses on these specific requirements, and thus measurably increases the opportunity for generating a favorable response from the employer.

Given this opportunity, however, I am always amazed how many applicants fail to take full advantage of this and continue to respond to advertisements using a general broadcast letter that fails to address the real needs of the employer. Such non-focused, general responses will normally fall short in addressing the specific requirements of the advertised position, leaving the employer to guess whether you have the qualifications desired. They can also suggest that your interest level is not sufficiently high for you to prepare an appropriate cover letter, or, worse yet, that you are simply too lazy to do so. Neither impression will aid your cause.

In many cases, you could be one of several hundred people who are responding to the ad. If, under these circumstances, you fail to tailor an appropriate cover letter that addresses specific requirements, you are placing yourself at a decided disadvantage compared to those who do so. Rather than highlighting those qualifications sought by the prospective employer and thereby increasing your chances of selection, you are solely relying on the employer to ferret out this information from the resume. In such cases, the employer may well decide to forgo your employment candidacy in favor of someone whose relevant qualifications for the position are clearly highlighted in the cover letter.

Why leave this matter to chance? If you are truly interested in the advertised position, it is strongly recommended that you take the time to carefully design an effective cover letter. By doing so, you substantially improve your chances of getting an employment interview.

Advertisement Analysis

The first step in designing an effective response to an employment advertisement is to study the ad to determine position requirements. The next step is to analyze your qualifications to determine which of the employer's requirements they meet. The cover letter will then be designed in such a way as to focus the reader's attention on the similarities between your specific qualifications and the stated requirements of the position—a comparison most employers will appreciate.

In order to facilitate the advertisement analysis process, I have provided the following set of questions that should prove helpful in getting the information you will need to prepare an effective cover letter and maximize your marketability.

1. What are the educational qualifications required for the position (i.e., degree level and major)? Describe below:

_____

_____

_____

2. What are your educational qualifications (i.e., degree level and major)? Describe below:

_____

_____

_____

3. What, if any, special skills training is required or preferred (beyond formal education)? Describe below:

_____

_____

_____

4. Have you had such special skills training? If so, describe the skill and the training you received.

_____

_____

_____

5. What specialized, technical or scientific knowledge does the position require (e.g., surface chemistry, statistical process control, salary surveys, Just-in-Time manufacturing)? List below:

_____

_____

_____

_____

_____

_____

6. In which of these areas are you knowledgeable? What evidence can you cite of your proficiency? Describe below:

_____

_____

_____

_____

_____

7. If a managerial position, what is the scope of experience required (functions managed, number of employees, budgets, etc.)? Describe below:

_____

_____

_____

_____

_____

_____

8. Which of these managerial experience requirements do you satisfy? Describe below:

_____

_____

_____

_____

_____

9. How many years of experience are required, and at what level? (By "level" I mean professional versus managerial level.) Describe below:

_____

_____

_____

10. How many years of experience do you have at these levels? Indicate below:

_____

_____

_____

11. What specific personal traits and characteristics are sought? List
     below:

_____

_____

_____

_____

12. Which of these personal traits and characteristics do you possess?
     Cite below:

_____

_____

_____

_____

This analysis will equip you to make a direct comparison between
the specific requirements of the employer, as stated in the ad, and your
own qualifications. This comparative information is then used as the
basis for your cover letter construction and ensures that this information will be readily available when needed.

Special Emphasis

Review of the specific wording chosen by the employer in an advertisement can often yield some tangible clues about qualifications that are
of particular interest. Most ads are slanted to emphasize the need for a
particular strength in a given area. Careful reading of the ad copy may
reveal what that area is.

Be alert for key words and phrases that are frequently used to convey
special interest in a particular area of qualification. Examples of such
key words and phrases are:

- Required.
- Is required.
- Must be.
- Must have.
- Must be capable of.
- Desirable.
- Very desirable.
- Must be thoroughly versed in/knowledgeable of.
- Should be strong in.

In addition to these special words or phrases, you should also be particularly alert for any repetition in the ad. If a specific qualification is repeated, you can bet the ranch that this is an area of particular interest to the employer. Such repetition usually means that the author of the advertisement wanted to make sure that this particular point was well covered, which, in turn, usually means that this is an area that will take on strong significance in the candidate selection process.

If you are able to discover a particular area of emphasis in the ad, be sure to take full advantage of it. If you have particularly strong qualifications in this special interest area, consider including in your cover letter a brief, separate paragraph that highlights those qualifications. If you are qualified in other areas specified as well, such a paragraph could well serve as a key factor in winning a personal interview.

Letter Components

Review of the sample cover letters at the end of this chapter will reveal that the advertising response cover letter contains certain standard components. These are, of course, in addition to the normal return address, date line, employer's address, and salutation. These components are as follows:

1. Reference to advertisement.
2. Expression of interest in position.
3. Comparison of position requirements with personal qualifications.

4. Statement of additional qualifications (optional).

5. Salary requirements statement (optional).

6. Geographical preference statement (optional).

7. Contact information.

8. Request for response or interview.

9. Statement of appreciation.

You will note that certain of these components are considered optional and may be either included in or excluded from the letter depending on how each adds or detracts from your overall candidacy. If you are adamant about compensation requirements or geographical considerations, then, by all means, include these items. Realize, however, that, as previously discussed, such inclusion will almost definitely have an adverse effect on your candidacy and, in certain circumstances, will cause you to be screened out from further employment consideration. Perhaps you may be better off excluding these items and reserving final judgment on compensation or location until after you have had the opportunity to consider the specifics of a given opportunity. The choice is yours.

The introductory paragraphs of the sample letters at the end of this chapter will reveal a specific mention of the position advertisement. Included in this reference are the name of the publication in which the ad appeared, the date of publication, and the position title, so that there is no confusion about the position for which you are applying. It should be pointed out that large companies, in particular, may be running simultaneous ads for numerous positions. Additionally, the advertisement response may, in some cases, be referred to different members of the employment function for review. If there is confusion in your letter as to the position, your letter and resume could well end up being reviewed by someone unfamiliar with the specifics of the position for which you are applying, which could prove fatal to your inquiry.

You will see that each of the sample cover letters at the end of this chapter also includes a specific statement of interest in the position for which the applicant is applying. Such interest statements should convey a sense of excitement and enthusiasm about the opening, which does not go unnoticed by the prospective employers and may serve to set your response apart from the hundreds of others they are likely to receive. In this regard, a little enthusiasm can go a long way toward creating interest in your candidacy.

Another standard feature of the advertising response cover letter is the comparison of your qualifications with the requirements stated in the ad. As the sample cover letters will attest, this comparison can use either a linear (line comparison) or a literary (paragraph comparison) approach. Either way, if done effectively, it can be a very powerful tool in leading the employer to the conclusion that you are well qualified for the position and deserving of an interview. Effective qualifications comparison is clearly the key factor in designing an impactful advertising response cover letter and thus deserves special attention.

The remaining components of the advertising response cover letter (i.e., contact information, request for response or interview, and statement of appreciation) have already been fully discussed in previous chapters and will not be discussed here.

The Linear Comparison

When using the linear comparison, the general approach is to begin by stating your belief that you are qualified for the position. This statement is then followed by line-by-line delineation of your qualifications that directly relate to the specific requirements contained in the advertisement. The following are some examples of the linear comparison technique:

Example A

Careful review of your requirements suggests that I am well qualified for the position of Materials Control Manager. Please consider the following:

1. *M.B.A. degree with materials management emphasis.*
2. *Ten years materials flow experience.*
3. *Three years materials control management with Fortune 200 company.*
4. *Thoroughly trained in JIT applications.*
5. *Heavily experienced in "total quality" vendor qualification methods.*
6. *Eight years experience in the consumer products industry.*

Example B

My credentials would appear to be an exact fit for the position of Director of Corporate Employment, as described in your advertisement. Please consider the following:

1. *M.B.A. from Cornell University.*
2. *B.S. degree in Industrial Management.*
3. *Twenty years Fortune 500 employment experience, 8 in corporate employment.*
4. *Six years employment management experience.*
5. *Senior level management recruitment experience.*
6. *Extensive use of executive search firms.*
7. *Management of high-volume technical recruitment in electronics industry.*

In each example, the factors listed in the linear comparison address a specific requirement listed by the employer in the advertisement. Further examples of the linear comparison are contained in the sample cover letters at the end of this chapter.

Generally, I recommend the linear comparison over the literary comparison, particularly when the employment applicant has most or all of the qualifications called for in the ad. This line-by-line description of qualifications is easily read and greatly facilitates qualifications comparison.

Let's now take a look at the literary comparison approach.

The Literary Comparison

The literary approach is recommended when only some of the employer's requirements are met. In such cases, use of the linear comparison will tend to make it too easy for the employer to spot the missing qualifications. Under these circumstances, the literary approach will better suit your purposes.

When using the literary comparison, you repeat a portion of the advertisement in the cover letter and then follow with a short description of your related qualifications. This approach facilitates comparison with requirements set forth in the recruitment ad and serves to highlight your qualifications to fill the position.

The following are some examples of the literary comparison approach:

Example A

Your ad states that you are seeking a "Ph.D. statistician with over 10 years of experience in the field of total quality." I hold a Ph.D. in Statistics from Washington University and have been employed by Radnor Corporation in the field of total quality for the last 12 years. Currently, I am the Manager of Total Quality for the corporation.

Example B

According to your ad, you are seeking a "Senior Project Engineer with a degree in Mechanical Engineering and over 8 years experience in paper machine project engineering."

I have an M.S. in Mechanical Engineering from the University of Michigan, and have been employed in the capacity of paper machine project engineer with Deltar Paper Company since 1991. During this time, I have played a primary role in the installation and/or rebuild of 6 paper machines. My last project entailed a $23 million rebuild of a light weight coated paper machine to include state-of-the-art, on-line coating technology.

The balance of this chapter contains several examples of employment advertisements, along with sample responses. You will note how these letters employ the comparison techniques just discussed, along with the other letter components discussed earlier.

Careful study of these letters and the recommendations made in this chapter should enable you to construct good cover letters that effectively respond to employment advertising and that enhance the probability of employment interviews.

SAMPLE A   *Employment Advertisement*

DIRECTOR OF
TOTAL QUALITY

Fortune 200 leader in the manufacture of printing and converting papers seeks Director of Total quality for its Chicago-based headquarters.

Position reports to President and will function as an in-house consulting resource to the senior executive staff, six operating divisions, and field sales organization in the development and implementation of a corporate-wide total quality initiative.

Position requires advanced Statistics degree and intimate knowledge of Deming's management principles and total quality methods. Successful candidates must be thoroughly versed in the application of statistics to TQM including design of experiments, control charting, variance analysis, etc.

Qualified candidates will have demonstrated expertise in the design and delivery of TQM statistical methods workshops at all organizational levels—hourly employee through executive. Preferred candidate will have successfully led implementation of a major TQM initiative in a sizeable organizational unit.

Interested persons send resume and compensation requirements to:

Mr. David R. Baxter
Director of Staffing
Fairfax Paper Company
825 Commerce Blvd.
Chicago, IL 18736

An Equal Opportunity Employer M/F

SAMPLE A   *Advertisement Response*

120 Sparrow Lane
Thorndale, PA 19274
March 24, 1998

Mr. David R. Baxter
Director of Staffing
Fairfax Paper Company
825 Commerce Boulevard
Chicago, IL 18736

Dear Mr. Baxter:

I am enclosing my resume in response to your March 23rd advertisement in the Chicago Tribune for a Director of Total Quality. This position sounds like an excellent match for my background and interest, and I would welcome the opportunity to discuss it further with you.

My matching qualifications are as follows:

- Ph.D. in Statistics from the University of Florida
- Dr. W. Edwards Deming Institute Graduate (1992)
- Successful design/implementation of Corporate TQM Program at Wesson Foods
- Expert in application of TQM statistical methods (e.g., experimental design, control charting, Paredo analysis, variance analysis, regression analysis, etc.)
- Designed/delivered 12-course series in TQM methods and statistics to over 6,000 employees (hourly workers, professionals, managers and executives) across corporation.

Should you agree that my credentials are a suitable match for your requirements, I would greatly appreciate the chance to further explore this opportunity through a personal interview. I feel confident that I can provide the kind of leadership that will ensure the success of your TQM initiative.

Salary requirements are in the low $100,000 range with some flexibility for negotiation dependent upon specifics of the offer and career growth prospects.

You can reach me during the day, on a confidential basis, at (215) 344-9586.

Thank you for your consideration, and I look forward to hearing from you.

Sincerely,

Barbara A. Bowman

Barbara A. Bowman

bab

Enclosure

SAMPLE B   *Employment Advertisement*

SENIOR PROJECT ENGINEERS PAPER MACHINES

Bramson Paper Company, a leading forest products company, seeks several project engineers to staff a $1.2 billion capital expansion project, the largest such project ever undertaken in company history. Successful candidates will have complete project responsibility from feasibility study through machine start up. This is an exciting opportunity for those seeking major project experience and accountability.

Positions require a B.S. in Mechanical Engineering plus five or more years experience in paper machine project engineering. Twin-wire forming and wet end experience highly desirable. Must be able to work independently, handle major project accountability, and provide technical direction to junior engineering staff. Familiarity with TDC 3000 control systems also desirable.

Excellent growth potential for advancement into engineering management. Highly competitive compensation and benefits package provided.

Qualified candidates should submit resume, including salary requirements, to:

Ms. Ann L. Johnson
Manager of Technical Staffing
Bramson Paper Company
200 East River Street
Dansford, MA 89372

An Equal Opportunity Employer M/F

SAMPLE B   *Advertisement Response*

Apt. 2-C, Lakeview Arms
200 Shore Road
Detroit, MI 29874
May 26, 1999

Ms. Ann L. Johnson
Manager of Technical Staffing
Bramson Paper Company
200 East River Street
Dansford, MA 89372

Dear Ms. Johnson:

You have piqued my interest with your May 24th <u>Boston Globe</u> advertisement for Senior Project Engineers—Paper Machines. This position sounds intriguing, and I therefore enclose my resume for your consideration. It appears that my qualifications and interest are both well-suited to your needs.

Your ad calls for a B.S. in Mechanical Engineering with over five years paper machine project experience. You state that twin-wire forming and wet-end experience are also desirable. I hold a B.S. degree in Mechanical Engineering from Michigan Technological University and have six years paper machine project engineering experience with Appleton Paper Company. This includes twin-wire forming. I have successfully engineered the complete forming section, including all wet-end systems, for a new 280" fine paper machine. All work was completed on time and under budget!

As called for in your ad, I have worked independently on major projects (up to $60 million) and have led project teams of up to six engineers. I also have extensive control systems background.

I appear well qualified for your opening, and would welcome the opportunity to further discuss the requirements in greater detail with you and the members of your engineering staff.

Compensation requirements are somewhat flexible; however, my current annual compensation is $90,000.

Since I travel and may be somewhat difficult to reach, please leave a phone mail message to include a convenient time for me to reach you. My phone number is (315) 344-9827.

Thank you for your consideration, and I look forward to hearing from you shortly.

Sincerely,

John C. Baker

jcb

Enclosure

SAMPLE C   *Employment Advertisement*

OPERATIONS MANAGER

Leading engineering firm in the asbestos abatement industry ($200 million sales) seeks talented Operations Manager for Southern New Jersey site. Position reports to Vice President of Consulting Engineering and is responsible for direction of 120-employee asbestos consulting and removable operations.

Position requires undergraduate engineering degree with 10+ years engineering construction management or allied experience. Must have solid experience in construction estimating and management of subcontract operations related to commercial and industrial structures. Knowledge of asbestos abatement and/or hazardous waste disposal helpful, but not required.

Our firm is experiencing dynamic growth and offers excellent career advancement opportunities for strong contributors.

Highly competitive compensation package along with exceptional flexible benefits package offered. Full relocation assistance available.

Send resume and compensation requirements to:

Christopher B. Waters
Human Resources Manager
Waste Disposal, Inc.
100 Lancaster Road
Wilmington, DE 17395

Equal Opportunity Employer M/F

SAMPLE C   *Advertisement Response*

200 Furling Lane
Annapolis, MD 13749
April 25, 1998

Mr. Christopher B. Waters
Human Resources Manager
Waste Disposal, Inc.
100 Lancaster Road
Wilmington, DE 17395

Dear Mr. Waters:

I read your April 24th ad for an Operations Manager in the <u>New York Times</u> with a great deal of interest. Please consider me a candidate for this position. A copy of my resume is enclosed for your reference.

It would appear that my background and experience are an excellent match for your needs, as demonstrated by the following highlights:

- B.S. degree in Civil Engineering from Drexel University
- 15 years engineering construction/consulting experience (8 years in construction)
- Large-scale commercial/industrial subcontract management experience (engineering of $30 to $40 million HVAC projects using 100 to 200 subcontract employees)
- Knowledge of chemical hazardous waste disposal

I have watched the impressive growth of the hazardous waste engineering/consulting industry, and am excited with the prospects of joining an organization such as yours. I hope to have the opportunity to meet with you personally to further explore career possibilities at Waste Disposal, Inc.

My current annual compensation at Colmar Engineering is $85,000. I would require compensation in the $90,000 to $95,000 range.

I can be reached at (412) 854-9725 during the day, or (412) 355-9827 during evening hours.

Thank you for your consideration, and I look forward to hearing from you in the near future.

Sincerely,

Wilma A. Davidson

Wilma A. Davidson

wad

Enclosure

SAMPLE D   *Employment Advertisement*

HUMAN RESOURCES MANAGER

Fortune 100 consumer products company seeks manager for Corporate Human Resources function. Reporting to the Vice President, position has functional responsibility for organization design & development, human resources planning, staffing, and compensation & benefits. Will manage staff of 42 professionals and provide full range of human resource services to 1,300 employee headquarters facility.

Successful candidate will have a Masters degree in Human Resources Management and 15 ears broad generalist experience. Must come from sizeable organization and led cultural transition from traditional management system to one that is participatory, team-based. Requires skilled facilitator capable of providing leadership to executive staff in innovating organizational change and new direction.

Position requires strong belief and advocacy for the fundamental principles of employee participation and "high-performance work systems". Must be an open, friendly, warm, easily approachable individual who engenders trust and confidence in others.

Highly competitive compensation package includes base salary plus performance bonus. Excellent benefits program.

Qualified individuals send complete resume, including compensation requirements to:

Sandra F. Jenkins
Vice President Human Resources
Bellstar Corporation
126 East 32nd Street
San Francisco, CA 64892

An Equal Opportunity Employer M/F

SAMPLE D   *Advertisement Response*

22 Ducktail Ridge
Roanoke, VA 13928
June 20, 1998

Ms. Sandra F. Jenkins
Vice President Human Resources
Bellstar Corporation
126 East 32nd Street
San Francisco, CA 64892

Dear Ms. Jenkins:

It is with great interest that I enclose my resume for the position of Human Resources Manager as advertised in the Wall Street Journal on June 19th. This appears an exciting career opportunity, and I would welcome the chance to meet with you to discuss the contributions I can make to your organization. I believe I am well qualified for this position.

Your ad states you seek an advanced Human Resources degree and 15+ years as a generalist in a major organization. You also require a skilled facilitator who strongly advocates the fundamental principles of employee participation and high-performance work systems, and who can provide senior management leadership in innovating organizational change processes.

I hold an M.S. in Industrial Relations from Michigan State University and have major company experience as a generalist. As Human Resources Manager for the Hilmarr Corporation, a $750 million (12,000 employees) electronic components manufacturer, I provide the full range of Human Resource services to the corporate staff and four operating divisions. I also serve as the senior O.D. consultant to the President's staff in change management, with focus on transforming the organization to a team-based, high-performance work system environment. I am the lead corporate advocate for employee participation, and we have made enormous inroads on several fronts!

Addressing some of the personal trait preferences described in your ad, I am known for being outgoing and personable in my approach. I have excellent rapport with employees, and believe they would describe me as both open and honest. I feel the "trust factor" would also be rated very high, and further believe that employees feel quite free to seek my counsel on sensitive matters.

I feel that I am an excellent match for your requirements, and would welcome the chance to further explore this opportunity with you directly. Compensation requirements are in the low $100,000 range.

Thank you for your consideration, and I look forward to hearing from you.

Sincerely,

Arthur D. Tailor

Arthur D. Tailor

adt

Enclosure

SAMPLE E   *Employment Advertisement*

COST ACCOUNTANT

A leader in the manufacture of industrial heat exchangers, Kelso Corporation is seeking a Manufacturing Cost Accountant for its Lawndale plant. This position reports to the Plant Accounting Manager and is accountable for all cost accounting for our Sun King industrial blower line. Kelso's sales have tripled in the past five years, and major expansion is planned.

We seek a person with a B.S. in Accounting and at least two years manufacturing cost experience. Prefer metal fabrication industry experience, but not an absolute requirement. Must be thoroughly versed in standard cost methodology and Lotus 1-2-3 or similar software. IBM compatible PC literacy a must.

Excellent salary and fringe benefits offered.

Send resume in confidence to:

Conwell R. Leinbach
Employment Manager
Kelso Corporation
1325 Wexler Street
Philadelphia, PA 19113

An Equal Opportunity Employer

SAMPLE E   *Advertisement Response*

205 Sail Road
Brigantine, NJ 15396
July 22, 1999

Mr. Conwell R. Leinbach
Employment Manager
Kelso Corporation
1325 Wexler Street
Philadelphia, PA 19113

Dear Mr. Leinbach:

I am forwarding my resume in response to your July 20th ad in the <u>Philadelphia Inquirer</u> for a Cost Accountant. I am very interested in this position, and would appreciate your consideration of my candidacy.

You will note from the enclosed resume that I have many of the attributes you are seeking for this position. Please consider the following:

- B.S. in Accounting from Penn State University (honors graduate)
- 3 years manufacturing cost accounting experience with ColdStar Corporation (an air conditioning metal cabinet fabricator)
- Thoroughly versed in standard manufacturing cost methodology
- Proficient in use of PC's, Lotus 1-2-3 and other spreadsheet software

For performance purposes, I have been consistently rated at the "exceeds all job requirements" level, and can furnish both strong business and personal references. I am noted for being unusually hard working, and enjoy an excellent reputation for the timeliness and accuracy of my work.

I would be very pleased to discuss your requirements in greater detail during a personal interview, and hope that I will have the opportunity to do so.

I can be confidentially reached during the day at (609) 426-3847 or at (609) 226-9384 during the evening.

Thank you for considering me, and I look forward to hearing from you in the near future.

Sincerely,

June C. Carver

June C. Carver

jcc

Enclosure

SAMPLE F   *Employment Advertisement*

CORPORATE BUYER
INDUSTRIAL CHEMICALS

National Foam, an $875 million leading manufacturer of polyurethane foams for industrial applications, seeks a Corporate Buyer for industrial chemicals. This is a centralized Procurement function supplying five plants, with annual chemicals budget of $125 million.

We seek a buyer with a B.S. degree in the chemical sciences, having 10+ years bulk industrial chemicals purchasing experience. Must be skillful negotiator of long-term bulk contracts with solid reputation for cost savings, quality, and on-time delivery. TDI, resins, or related experience helpful, but not required. Must be intimately familiar with bulk purchasing and multi-location delivery.

Excellent compensation and benefits package is available for qualified candidates. Relocation assistance also provided.

Jeffrey A. Morse
Director of Human Resources
National Foam, Inc.
100 Henderson Road
Old Forge, NY 89573

We Are An Equal Opportunity Employer

SAMPLE F   *Advertisement Response*

18 Kilmer Lane
Rome, NY 12847
August 21, 1998

Mr. Jeffrey A. Morse
Director of Human Resources
National Foam, Inc.
100 Henderson Road
Old Forge, NY 89573

Dear Mr. Morse:

Your August 20th ad in the <u>Rochester Herald</u> for a Corporate Buyer - Industrial Chemicals caught my eye! This position appears an excellent fit for my background, and I am enclosing my resume in hopes that I can generate an equal level of interest in my candidacy.

Your ad indicates you are looking for a science-degreed chemical buyer with 10+ years industrial bulk chemical procurement experience for a multi-location company. You state you require a skilled, long-term bulk chemical contract negotiator with a reputation for cost savings, quality and on-time delivery. This seems to fit me to a "Tee"!

A degreed chemist, I have been employed as a bulk chemical buyer by the Buttal Corporation for over 12 years. My forte has been successful negotiation of some $85 million of long-term bulk chemical contracts for multi-locations (3 plants) at very favorable terms and pricing.

By centralizing chemical buying and negotiating improved long-term, bulk contracts, I have saved Buttal over $6 million annually, and greatly improved both quality and delivery service to our manufacturing sites. Through my efforts, we have also built stronger partnerships with our suppliers which have, in fact, led to product improvements that have enhanced our competitiveness in the marketplace.

I am quite interested in the position you advertised, and would welcome the chance to further explore this opportunity during a personal interview. I feel I can contribute significantly to your objectives, improving both cost and service to your organization.

Please feel free to contact me at (315) 775-0937 during the day or at (315) 644-9284, which is my home number, during the evening.

I would be pleased to hear from you. Thank you for your consideration.

Sincerely,

Scott M. Beatty

Scott M. Beatty

smb

Enclosure

SAMPLE G   *Employment Advertisement*

Senior Research Scientist

Leading Fortune 50 chemical company headquartered in Wilmington, Delaware seeks talented Senior Research Scientist for its Agricultural Chemicals Division Research Team. Position reports to the Director of Process Development, and will serve as lead scientist in the development of an oxidation process for a new herbicide intermediate with potential production of several million pounds per year.

This position requires a Ph.D. in Organic Chemistry and at least 5 years research experience in the development of agricultural chemicals, including production scale-up of herbicides. Requires creative problem-solver with strong communications and team skills. Must have a demonstrated track record of successful new product development and be skilled at both pilot plant trials and full scale start-up.

Position offers highly competitive base salary plus performance-based incentives. Generous benefits program, including company-paid medical coverage for both employee and dependents.

Qualified candidates, please send or email your resume, including compensation requirements to:

Wilma R. Stevenson
Director of Staffing
Horton Chemical Company
116 East Market Street
Wilmington, DL 18374

Email: WilSte@Horton.com

An Equal Opportunity Employer

SAMPLE G   *Advertisement Response*

818 Kimberly Lane
West Chester, PA 19382
December 4, 2005

Ms. Wilma R. Stevenson
Director of Staffing
Horton Chemical Company
116 East Market Street
Wilmington, DL 18374

Dear Ms. Stevenson:

In opening the December 3rd edition of the *Wilmington Times,* I was delighted to find your advertisement for a Senior Research Scientist, a position that appears an excellent fit for my credentials. This position is of particular interest to me, and I am therefore enclosing my resume for your consideration.

As called for in your ad, I hold a Ph.D. in Organic Chemistry from the University of Delaware and have over 5 years in agricultural chemicals process development, including both pilot plant development work and full-scale start-up experience. As a Senior Scientist for Agri Chemicals, Inc., I have been instrumental in the development of a number of new products and processes, including work with herbicides.

My creativity is supported by the fact that, as the principal scientist in each case, I have been issued 12 U.S. patents for new chemical processes and products. I have excellent communications skills and function extremely effectively as both a leader and key contributor to product development teams.

Several of my key accomplishments have been detailed on the attached resume. I think you will find that my qualifications are an excellent match for your requirements, and that I would be capable of making an immediate contribution to your new herbicide process development program.

If you agree, I would welcome a phone call (or email) to see if we can arrange a convenient time to meet to further discuss my background and this interesting employment opportunity. I can be reached at my office phone, (302) 557-9574.

Thank you, and I look forward to hearing from you.

Sincerely,

Carla P. Swenson

Carla P. Swenson

SAMPLE H   *Employment Advertisement*

Product Manager
Marketing

Leading, $8 billion, Fortune 100 forest products company seeks talented Product Manager – Marketing for its Plywood & Lumber Products Division. This position reports to the Vice President of Marketing and is accountable for development and implementation of brand strategies designed to further penetrate and expand market share for its new line of pressed composite board sold into world markets through an international distributor network.

Successful candidates will possess an M.B.A. in Marketing from a top school, and at least 6 years brand management experience in the forest products industry to include marketing of lumber products. Must demonstrate strong strategic thinking skills, and have solid, in-depth knowledge of the market and key competitors. Also requires demonstrated success in the launch and establishment of brand leadership for new product lines.

Excellent advancement opportunities based upon contribution and accomplishment. Competitive base salary combined with attractive incentive program. Full benefits program provided.

Qualified candidates, please forward full resume and compensation requirements to:

Arnold W. Bresner
Staffing Manager

Wilson Forest Products, Inc.
835 Commerce Way, Green Bay, WI 18374

An Equal Opportunity Employer

SAMPLE H *Advertisement Response*

926 Pine Ridge Trail
Federal Way, WA 23847
November 16, 2003

Mr. Arnold W. Bresner
Staffing Manager
Wilson Forest Products, Inc.
835 Commerce Way
Green Bay, WI 18374

Dear Mr. Bresner:

Your advertisement for Product Manager - Marketing appearing in the current issue of *Forest Products News* caught my eye. As the enclosed resume will confirm, I appear to be exceptionally well qualified for this position and would welcome the chance to further explore this opportunity during a personal interview at your headquarters in Green Bay.

Please consider the following brief summary of relevant qualifications:

- M.B.A. in Marketing from the University of Chicago
- 7 years Brand Management experience in the Forest Products Industry
- 3 years marketing accountability for plywood and wood flooring products
- Led brand strategy that propelled new brand from # 6 to # 2 in market share in 3 years
- Successfully launched 4 new wood product lines, consistently beating market share objectives

My entire career has been with the Wood Products Division of Rainier Forest Products Company, where I have distinguished myself as a major contributor to its corporate marketing function.

Should you agree that my qualifications are a good match for your current staffing need, I would appreciate hearing from you in the near future. You need to be aware that I am currently under serious consideration for a Senior Brand Manager's position with another company, and anticipate receiving an offer in the near future.

The position of Product Manager - Marketing at Wilson sounds quite appealing, however, and I would hope to have the chance to discuss this opportunity with you shortly.

Thank you for your consideration.

Sincerely,

Daniel C. Baker

Daniel C. Baker

Enclosure

10

NETWORKING COVER LETTERS

Over the years, there has been a considerable amount written about the importance of personal networking as a means to finding employment. Personal contact, or *networking,* still remains the number one employment source for finding a job, greatly outstripping all other methods.

Various studies have shown that, networking as a job-hunting methodology, counts for approximately 70 percent of all professional and managerial jobs that are found by job seekers. It also seems that the higher the level of the position sought, the more important the role played by networking in landing the job. A study recently released by Harvard Business School, for example, confirms this observation, suggesting that as high as 90 percent of all senior level executive positions are, in fact, filled through personal networking process.

This data seems to suggest that a good part of your job-search time and effort should be committed to the use of networking. It is believed that effective networking has the potential to cut job-hunting time by as much as 50 percent to 75 percent. Additionally, studies have shown that positions found through networking tend to pay higher and prove more rewarding and satisfying than those found using alternate job-hunting methods.

These are all good reasons for you to learn to become a highly effective networker, if your objective is to find a good job within a relatively short time frame.

What Is Networking and Why Does It Work So Well?

The general term *network* is normally defined as a "series of connected things." For example, a computer network is a series of computers hooked together into a system so that information can be shared between them. Through the network, then, the computer operator can access data from, or transmit data to, any or all of the other computers connected to the network.

Likewise, a social network is a group of people that are somehow connected or affiliated. They are generally connected for a common purpose or need. Most frequently, the reason for the connection is for either information or support. The objective of social networks can be either personal or business related. Personal networks are normally comprised of friends and acquaintances and are usually held together by common social and personal interests. Business networks, on the other hand, are generally joined together by the need to meet one or more business objectives or satisfy an operating need.

Social networks, both personal and business, are the heart of the job-search networking process. It is through these contacts (i.e., network members) that the job seeker works to identify employment opportunities. It is the objective of employment networking, therefore, to access these vital contacts for the purpose of asking their assistance in helping you find suitable employment. If approached properly, these contacts often have the potential to provide you with direct job leads or introduce you to others, in their own networks, who can be of assistance to you in finding satisfying employment.

The Multiplier Effect

An important phenomena that accounts for the huge success of employment networking is what is known as the *multiplier effect*. If you had only the ability to contact persons who you know "directly" (i.e., those who are members of your own personal or business network), the job-search networking process would likely meet with limited success. By asking your direct contacts to open up their social and business networks to you and pave the way for appropriate introductions, however, you suddenly have the potential to expand your contacts manyfold, essentially recruiting a large army of people who are willing to provide assistance to you with regard to your job search.

Further, by also tapping into the personal and business networks of these indirect networking contacts (i.e., those to whom your direct contacts introduced you), the whole process begins to multiply itself, exploding suddenly into a huge network of hundreds (if not thousands) of individuals committed to helping you identify job opportunities that may be of interest.

For those of you who have had a basic biology course, another way to visualize the dramatic impact of job-search networking is to think of the process of cell division. Organisms grow by multiplying their cells. Each organism starts as a single cell, which then divides in two. The resultant two cells than each again divide into another two cells (now a total of four cells). Each of these four cells then divides again into two more (now a total of eight cells). And so the process of cell division continues, eventually resulting in a complete organism comprised of thousands if not millions of individual cells.

The employment networking process is quite similar. Due to the multiplier effect of tapping into the networks of others, and then into the networks of those to whom you are subsequently introduced, you are quickly able to multiply a handful of initial contacts into a huge network of others who are willing, in some way or another, to help you with your job-hunting efforts.

The Obligation Phenomenon

Although I have just explained *how* networking works, I have yet to explain *why* it works so effectively. Although there are many nuances to successful networking, a fundamental element that accounts for its success is known as the *obligation phenomenon.*

At the heart of employment networking is the *personal referral process.* Each time you talk to a new networking contact, sometime during that conversation you will eventually want to get around to asking this contact for referral and/or introductions to others who are part of that contact's social and business networks. It is this very act of requesting such referrals that is the glue that holds the networking process together and causes it to work.

When placing subsequent calls to these new referral contacts, you are now in a position to tell them you have been referred by someone this new contact knows either socially or professionally. The fact that such a social or business relationship with the referring source exists, creates a natural sense of "obligation" to respond to you in a positive way. Although there is certainly no absolute obligation to so respond, the basic laws of society suggests that positive or helpful response is both appropriate and expected. To do otherwise would represent an affront and potentially jeopardize one's relationship with the individual making the referral.

Using a Networking Cover Letter

One way to make networking calls (or personal meetings with networking contacts) more productive is through the use of a well-written networking cover letter. Such letters may be sent either via e-mail or "snail mail" to the networking contact in advance of your contact with them. These letters to accomplish three primary objectives:

1. Set the stage for a personal introduction.
2. Pave the way for a phone conversation or personal meeting.
3. Transmit your resume, familiarizing the networking contact with your background and qualifications in advance of your discussion.

Review of the sample cover letters that follow will show that effective networking cover letters typically incorporate certain key elements. These are as follow:

1. Personal opening.
   a. Name of person making the referral.
   b. Relationship to you (optional).
   c. Some personal comments (where appropriate).
2. Explanation of how referral occurred (optional).
3. Reason for job change (optional).
4. Reference to specific, known job opening (if one exists).
5. Indirect approach (where no known job opening exists).
6. Reference to enclosed resume.
7. Action statement designed to arrange direct contact (i.e., meeting or phone call).
8. Thank you.

If carefully written, the employment-networking letter can be a very effective tool. It makes use of personal ties and relationships to systematically and greatly expand your circle of contacts, directly involving legions of others in helping you with your job search and opening numerous doors to key contacts that would otherwise be closed to you. Since the networking cover letter sets the stage for these valuable introductions, it is important that it be carefully crafted and written well.

The following pages contain sample networking cover letters that you will find easy to adopt in tailoring your own letters in support of your job-search networking efforts.

SAMPLE A   *Employment Networking Letter*

614 Fleming Road
Canton, OH 13247
April 7, 2004

Ms. Nancy A. Davidson
Director of Sales & Marketing
Baxter Companies, Inc.
217 Industrial Highway
Cleveland, OH 15249

Dear Nancy:

Walt Brunson and I are close friends, and I am writing to you at his suggestion. We have adjoining boat slips at The Sailing Emporium and have known one another for a number of years. I understand from Walt that you are a sailor as well and have been known to frequent Annapolis Harbor from time to time. It is a wonder that our paths haven't crossed, since I have spent many a summer weekend tied up in one of the slips at the town dock.

Last week, during a sailing trip to Baltimore Inner Harbor, I mentioned to Walt that I had decided to make a career move. Since my background is in Sales and Marketing, he suggested that I might want to touch base with you to see if you might have some thoughts on this matter. Any general thoughts or ideas you could share with me would be very much appreciated.

As you can see from the enclosed resume, I hold an M.B.A. in Marketing from Ohio State University and have had a successful career in the Sales and Marketing field. Most recently, I have been National Accounts Manager for Thornton Industries, a leading manufacturer of specialty chemicals sold to the pharmaceutical industry. Unfortunately, Royal Chemical recently bought Thornton, and they will be installing their own management team.

According to Walt, your firm is a supplier to a number of specialty chemical companies. Perhaps, through your contacts in the field, you may be aware of someone currently looking for a National Accounts Manager or Senior Sales Representative. If not, perhaps you could suggest some key contacts through whom I might network. Either way, I would appreciate any thoughts or ideas you might have on the matter.

I will be in Cleveland the week of April 26 and, if your schedule permits, perhaps we could meet over lunch or dinner. I will give you a call later this week to see if we can get together. In the meantime, the enclosed resume will provide you with a broader view of my professional experience and credentials.

Thank you for your help, Nancy, and I look forward to the possibility of meeting with you during my forthcoming trip to the Cleveland area.

Sincerely,

David R. Wilson

David R. Wilson

rjt

Enclosure

SAMPLE B   *Employment Networking Letter*

120 Greenfield Circle
Augusta, GA 13296
July 22, 2005

Mr. George T. Culver
Corporate Director
Research & Development
Bristol Laboratories, Inc.
204 Bristol Way
Ashville, NC 13827

Dear George:

It seems we have a mutual friend. Dave Baxter and I are fraternity brothers from our college days at Georgia Tech. About four years ago, while playing singles in a local tennis tournament, we discovered that we have been living in the same town. We have since teamed up and are playing as doubles partners in the Augusta Seniors Tournament. No championships yet!

While at dinner on Saturday evening, I mentioned to Dave I was seriously considering a career change. Due to major cuts in Seneca Laboratories' research budget, it appears that things are on a downward slide and future opportunities for advancement and career growth are looking dim. As a result, I have reluctantly concluded I need to move on.

Dave tells me Bristol Laboratories is contemplating expansion of its research facilities and may possibly be in the market for a Principal Scientist in absorbent research. Since this is my area of specialty, he suggested I contact you, thinking there may be a possible match. As the enclosed resume indicates, I hold a Ph.D. in Materials Science and have nearly ten years experience as a research scientist in absorbent structures.

I am planning a trip to Ashville in the next few weeks and would love the opportunity to meet with you. Although interested in opportunities at Bristol, should there not be an appropriate position at this time, I would still value any general ideas or advice you might have regarding my job search. Perhaps there are others who you know in the research community who might prove valuable as networking contacts. I would be grateful for any thoughts or advice you might provide.

I will call later this week to see if your schedule will permit us to get together. My timing is fairly flexible, and I would be pleased to make the necessary adjustments to allow us to meet.

My sincere thanks for your help in this matter.

Sincerely,

Kevin Murphy

Kevin R. Murphy

dmt

Enclosure

SAMPLE C *Employment Networking Letter*

621 Mountain Way
Seattle, WA 14386
May 28, 2006

Ms Wilma A. Reismiller
Director of Human Resources
Delmar Corporation
215 Dupont Highway
Wilmington, DE 19327

Dear Wilma:

I am writing at the suggestion of Sam Jackson, a friend and former neighbor here in Seattle. Sam, as you know, was transferred to the Philadelphia area last year by his company, and tells me that he has gotten to know you through serving together on the Program Committee of the Wilmington Area Chamber of Commerce. I believe he mentioned me to you during your last Committee meeting.

Wilma, I am a graduate of Drexel University and a former Philadelphia native, who would like to return to the Philadelphia Area. I have elderly parents still residing in the area and, considering the distance, am finding it difficult to provide for their needs. I am sure you can appreciate the special challenge this presents.

As the enclosed resume shows, I have an M.S. in Industrial Psychology from Drexel and nearly fifteen years experience in the Human Resources field, with emphasis on Labor Relations. I am seeking a senior level position that will make effective use of my labor management skills.

Although you might not be aware of a specific opportunity for me, as a senior level HR professional who is active in the Philadelphia area HR community, I thought perhaps you might be in a position to provide some general thoughts and suggestions on how I might go about networking in the local area. Additionally, I would appreciate any other thoughts or ideas you might have concerning my job search.

Wilma, I will plan to give you a call in the next few days and would sincerely appreciate any assistance you might be able to provide to me in this matter.

Thank you, and I look forward to speaking with you.

Sincerely,

Donna Wexler

Donna B. Wexler

wjm

Enclosure

SAMPLE D   *Employment Networking Letter*

114 East Windsor Way
Windsor Locks, CT 13295
February 18, 2005

Ms Katherine W. Lewis
Mortgage Loan Officer
Connecticut Bank & Trust
122 Commercial Way
Hartford, CT 13286

Dear Katherine:

I am always surprised at what a small world it is! Last Saturday, while shopping at Dreifords at the Enfield Mall, I ran into Marshall Tailor, a former high school classmate from Springfield High. During our conversation, your name came up, and Marshall mentioned that the two of you were in several classes together while at Springfield Community College and continue to maintain a close friendship.

When I mentioned to Marshall that I was seeking a position in Commercial Banking, he immediately thought of you and suggested I give you a call. As it turns out, I already had your name on a short list of key banking contacts, to which I was planning to write.

Katherine, as I am sure you are aware, Boston Financial recently acquired Springfield Federal, and has proceeded to lay off over 50% of Springfield's corporate officers. Unfortunately, as Springfield's Commercial Loan Officer, my position has been eliminated, and I am now in search of a new opportunity. I have taken the liberty of enclosing a copy of my resume for your reference.

Rather than simply write, Marshall suggested that I also give you a call and mention that he referred me to you. I was hoping that I might buy lunch and seek your general thoughts and ideas concerning my career transition. Perhaps you could suggest some key networking contacts in the banking community who might be helpful in identifying a suitable career opportunity.

Katherine, I would greatly appreciate any ideas or help you could provide and will call you to see if you could spare some time to meet with me.

Thank you.

Sincerely,

Dave Cooper

David W. Cooper

Enclosure

SAMPLE E   *Employment Networking Letter*

16 College Avenue
Turtle Rock, CA 14237
September 4, 2006

Mr. Carlton B. Foster
Chief Financial Officer
Vartec Technology, Inc.
1824 McArthur Blvd.
Irvine, CA 19238

Dear Carlton:

Yesterday, I ran into Jim Smith while having dinner at Fosters in Laguna Beach. Jim mentioned that he knew you from Rotary and suggested I contact you. He said to tell you that he is still up for that golf match that the two of you need to get on your schedules.

Carlton, the reason for Jim's suggestion that I contact you has to do with my recent decision to make a career change. Since I also work in Finance for a local technology company, it seemed to make sense for me to give you a call. I have enclosed a copy of my resume to provide you with an overview of my credentials.

I am hopeful that you might have time to grab some lunch or a cup of coffee together. I certainly don't expect you will be aware of a specific job opportunity for me, but I would greatly appreciate your general thoughts and counsel concerning my career search. Perhaps you may also be aware of others working in the Financial field who might be good persons for me to contact.

I will plan to give you a call early next week to see if we can plan a convenient time to get together.

Thank you, and I look forward to talking with you.

Sincerely,

Martha Billingsworth

Martha C. Billingsworth

Enclosure

SAMPLE F   *Employment Networking Letter*

421 Butterworth Lane
Springfield, MO 12332
April 22, 2004

Mr. Martin S. Bolinski
Chief Executive Officer
The Bower Corporation
122 Technology Way
Denver, CO 12837

Dear Martin:

Good friends are hard to find, but it appears we are fortunate to share one!

Walter Davis and I go back a long way. We served in the Gulf War as part of the 101st Airborne and shared a foxhole together just north of Kuwait during some of the heaviest fighting. Nothing like a life-threatening crisis, such as war, to bring two kindred souls together!

Since the war, we have stayed in close touch and spend a week's vacation together each year, either in Missouri or in Colorado. He has mentioned you to me on several occasions and has told me of the great times the two of you had growing up in the Denver area.

During a recent conversation with Walt, I mentioned that I was caught in a downsizing at the Warwick Company, where my job as Plant Manager was eliminated as part of the Company's decision to shut down the Springfield Plant. Although I was offered a comparable position in New York, my family and I have no desire to move to the East Coast. Colorado, however, is a different story!

Walt suggested I send my resume and give you a call. He is aware that you are President of the Denver Manufacturers' Association, and thought you might have some ideas or contacts that could be of help to me. I am planning to visit Walt next month and thought perhaps the three of us could get together. I will plan to give you a call, and see if we can set this up.

I have heard a lot about you (all very positive) and look forward to meeting you in person!

Sincerely,

Bill Thornton

William S. Thornton, III

Enclosure

SAMPLE G   *Employment Networking Letter*

106 Summit Avenue
Willingboro, NJ 18374
October 22, 2005

Ms. Linda A. Breckert
2002 Wylam Road
Springfield, PA 13849

Dear Linda:

Yesterday, during intermission at the Bach Concert series at the Kimmel Center in Center City, I ran into a mutual friend of ours, David Brownsteen. David and I were doubles partners in the Greater Delaware Valley Tennis Association's annual tournament two years ago, and have developed a close friendship. I understand from David that you are an avid tennis player yourself, and have won a number of tournaments in the region.

During the course of our conversation, I confidentially mentioned to David that I was considering a career change, and he strongly suggested I contact you, thinking you might be in a position to be of some assistance. I understand that you are a principal in an executive search firm with strong connections in the Pharmaceutical industry. Perhaps you could offer some pointers on how to best go about initiating my career search.

I am currently Regional Manager for Stanford Pharmaceuticals and manage a 6-state sales region in the Northeast covering the states of Pennsylvania, New Jersey, New York, Connecticut, Delaware, and Maryland. Although I have been in sales and sales management with Stanford for the last 12 years, recent acquisition of our company by Janzen Corporation has caused me to give serious consideration to making a career move. I have enclosed a copy of my resume for your reference.

I would greatly appreciate the opportunity to meet with you to discuss my situation, and to seek your general ideas and advice on an appropriate job-search strategy. David said you are an expert in this arena and would likely be able to steer me in the right direction.

Perhaps we could meet for lunch in the next week or so, your schedule permitting. I will give you a call in the next day or two to see if there is a convenient time for us to get together.

I look forward to meeting you, and would be most appreciative of any assistance you might provide.

Thank you.

Sincerely,

Wanda Jaimeson

Wanda Jaimeson

Enclosure

SAMPLE H   *Employment Networking Letter*

265 North Hanover Street
Syracuse, NY 13274
January 21, 2006

Mr. Leroy K. Jackson
Vice President – Logistics
The Cooper Company, Inc.
300 Industrial Highway, North
Binghamton, NY 13459

Dear Leroy:

On Tuesday of this week, Calvin Johnson and I ran into one another at the 30th Street Station in Philadelphia. It turned out that we were both headed for New York City, so we decided to sit together. Calvin and I are related through marriage. He is my wife's cousin, and we have seen one another on several occasions during family reunions.

During the course of our train conversation, I mentioned that I had just been caught as part of a reorganization and 8,000-employee downsizing by Pitney Bowes Corporation and was headed for a job interview with a search firm in New York City. When I mentioned that I had a strong management background in Logistics, Calvin suggested I contact you.

I understand that you are President of the New York Chapter of the American Logistics Association and are also quite active at the national level as well. Calvin seemed to feel you might be of some assistance in helping me with some key networking contacts and providing me with some ideas and general advice in connection with my job search.

I would be most appreciative of any assistance you might provide.

At Calvin's suggestion, I have enclosed a copy of my resume, providing a fairly thorough summary of my career and accomplishments to date. Hopefully this will provide you with a good synopsis of my credentials.

I will plan to call you early next week to see if there would be a convenient time for us to talk. I look forward to our conversation, and any thoughts you might have for me.

By the way, Calvin said to say "hello," and to let you know he will be in Binghamton next week, and would like to see if the two of you can get together for dinner.

Sincerely,

Arthur T. Lewis

Arthur T. Lewis

Enclosure

SAMPLE I   *Employment Networking Letter*

517 East Windsor Street
Portland, OR 21375
April 26, 2005

Ms. Veronica Meyers
Vice President of Development
The Breast Cancer Coalition
1805 Commerce Row
Seattle, WA 32859

Dear Vicki:

Perhaps you may recall, we briefly met at a Breast Cancer Coalition dinner and fundraiser last spring in Seattle, at which time we were introduced by our mutual friend, Cindy Davis. Cindy has often spoken of you, and the tremendous job you are doing in leading the Coalition's many fundraising events. You are certainly to be congratulated for your commitment and dedication to this worthy cause!

Vicki, during lunch conversation with Cindy last Tuesday, I mentioned that I was thinking about a career change, and felt I might enjoy being a professional fundraiser in the not-for-profit sector. I have strong sales and marketing skills and a keen interest in becoming a key member of a worthwhile community service organization.

In discussing the possibilities with Cindy, she immediately thought of you and felt you might be willing to meet with me to share some insights about the challenges and rewards of working in the world of professional fundraising. I can't think of a person better qualified to offer such advice!

I would certainly appreciate any guidance you might provide, and would very much appreciate if you could spare an hour or so to meet with me. Perhaps we could meet at Valentias for lunch.

I will plan to call you in the next day or so to see if you can find some time for me in that busy schedule of yours. Of course, lunch will be on me!

I look forward to speaking with you, and to the possibility of getting together.

Regards,

Susan Beekman

Susan Beekman

SAMPLE J   *Employment Networking Letter*

62 Winding Way
Nashville, TN 13285
September 19, 2004

Mr. Gerald R. Richter
Vice President of Project Engineering
Foster Engineering
1802 Vickers Street, SW
Nashville, TN 23185

Dear Gerry:

Last evening my neighbor, Steve Temple and I, were sitting on Steve's front porch discussing a number of topics, when the subject of work satisfaction came up. During this conversation, I shared with Steve that my current engineering project at Walden Papers is coming to an end, and that I am concerned about job stability. Walden has reported a loss for two consecutive quarters, and there appear to be no new capital projects being booked.

Steve said that during a recent conversation you mentioned Foster Engineering had landed a number of major projects, and was currently in the market to hire a number of System Engineers to support the increased project load. He strongly suggested that I contact you to explore the possibility of employment.

I have an M.S. degree in Electrical Engineering with an emphasis in Systems. For the last 8 years I have worked as a Senior Systems Engineer with responsibility for design and installation of manufacturing control systems in the paper industry. I am a skilled engineer with exposure to a wide range of control systems, including both process and motor controls.

I have taken the liberty of enclosing a copy of my resume, detailing the specifics of my background and credentials. Perhaps there may be a fit for one of your current openings.

Perhaps, even if there is no appropriate opening at Foster, you would be kind enough to meet with me to discuss my current situation. I would welcome any ideas and/or advice you might offer in connection with my job search.

I will plan to call your office shortly to see if we can arrange a convenient time to meet. Coffee is on me!

Thank you for your consideration, and I look forward to speaking with you.

Sincerely,

Craig T. Logan

Craig T. Logan

Enclosure

11

THE RESUME LETTER

The resume letter is not a true cover letter—that is, it is not a letter designed to simply transmit your resume to an employer. Instead, it is a letter that is intended to actually *replace* the resume, and to convey sufficient information about your qualifications to entice an employer to interview you.

In general, I am not a strong advocate of the resume letter and do not normally recommend its use. My views on this subject appear to be borne out by a recent survey of over 500 human resource professionals by the Society for Human Resource Management (SHRM), where a full 91 percent considered a "detailed job history" as either important or very important. A one-page resume letter hardly seems to meet this criterion.

Generally speaking, the resume letter does not typically provide sufficient information (when compared to the standard two-page resume) for the employer to make a reasonable assessment of the job seeker's qualifications and decide whether or not to grant an employment interview. In addition to the frustration it may cause the employer, it may also suggest that the applicant is either unable or too lazy to prepare a resume document. Thus, it is not likely to serve your best interests if you are truly interested in creating a favorable impression and persuading an employer to grant you an interview.

Despite these objections, we continue to see use of this approach by a small number of job seekers. To be complete, therefore, we want to give you examples of the best of this kind of letter.

It seems that the most frequent use of the resume letter is by senior level executives who wish simply to announce their availability and conduct a cursory search of the job market. Such letters are typically directed at the most senior levels of the target organization (e.g., board chairperson, president, chief executive officer, chief operating officer) and are intended to convey availability and general interest in discussing appropriate opportunities. The logic typically supporting use of such letters (versus the standard resume) is that the applicant's current position and employment speak for themselves, and there is therefore no need for a full-blown resume document. In many cases, where a resume letter is chosen, the job seeker works for a direct competitor, and his or her qualifications are obvious to the prospective employer.

If the job seeker works for a direct competitor or is employed in an officer-level position for a well-known Fortune 100 company, a resume letter may be sufficient to generate interest. However, where the job seeker is employed in a lower level position, or the employer is a little known company, the resume letter will not have the same effect. In such cases, I would strongly recommend use of the conventional resume document along with an appropriate cover letter.

The following are some examples of resume letters where the author is either working for a direct competitor of the company to whom the letter has been addressed or is employed in a fairly senior level capacity with a well-known company.

SAMPLE A   *Resume Letter (Direct Competitor)*

125 Bridle Path Lane
Wayne, PA 19274
July 16, 2004

Mr. Matthew R. Weyman
President
Larson Paper Company, Inc.
200 Commerce Drive
Appleton, WI 12837

Dear Mr. Weyman:

Recent changes in the composition of the Board of Directors of Warsaw Paper Company have caused me to rethink my career plans. I am therefore electing to confidentially explore outside opportunities. I am sure you can appreciate the sensitivity of this matter. My employer is unaware of this decision.

As Senior Vice President of Operations for Warsaw, I report to the President and am responsible for all company manufacturing operations. This entails management of 6 operating divisions, 24 manufacturing sites, and 32,000 employees spread over 3 continents and 16 countries. Under my leadership, manufacturing operations have returned a documented $300 million in cost savings during the last 5 years.

A Wharton-educated M.B.A., I have over 20 years of successful manufacturing and operations management experience with major U.S. corporations. My contributions to these firms have been significant and have resulted in rapid career advancement into the senior management ranks. I am now looking to further expand my career horizons.

Should you be aware of a suitable opportunity or should you be aware of others with whom I should be in contact in this regard, I would appreciate hearing from you. I can be reached, on a confidential basis, at (610) 557-9500.

Thank you for your consideration and assistance in this matter.

Sincerely,

Robert T. Barnesworth

Robert T. Barnesworth

ftg

SAMPLE B   *Resume Letter (Well-Known Company)*

2 Green Ridge Road
Schenectady, NY 12846
March 22, 2006

Mr. Stuart B. Kingsley
Chairman
Universal Systems, Inc.
300 Industrial Way
Baltimore, MD 19326

Dear Mr. Kingsley:

I have recently decided to initiate a career change and am now exploring career options in general management at the senior level. This inquiry is, of course, highly confidential since my company is unaware of my decision.

I am currently Vice President and General Manager of General Electric's Small Motors Division, where I report directly to the Senior Vice President of Operations for General Electric Corporate. In this capacity, I have P&L responsibility for a $6 billion, 28,000-employee division with 26 manufacturing facilities in 18 countries. I also serve on the Board of Directors of the Dexter Engineering Company, a $300 million company engaged in the design engineering of gas-fired utilities.

Although I have enjoyed my experience at General Electric and have been treated well, future growth opportunities appear limited, and I now have a strong desire to affiliate with a smaller, entrepreneurial, high-growth company, where my executive and leadership talents can be more fully utilized. I am therefore seeking a position as CEO or President of a firm meeting this profile.

In addition to my extensive experience in operations and general management, my credentials include an M.B.A. from Harvard Business School and a B.S. degree in Mechanical Engineering from Cornell, where I graduated with honors.

Mr. Kingsley, should you be aware of a suitable executive opportunity, I would very much appreciate a call. I can be reached at (503) 667-9500.

Thank you for your assistance in this matter.

Sincerely,

Gwendolyn P. Bradson

Gwendolyn P. Bradson

pds

12

EMPLOYMENT THANK
YOU LETTERS

No book on cover letters or employment letters would be complete without covering the topic of thank you letters.

As an employment professional, I am amazed at the number of job seekers who never think to send a basic thank you letter to employers following a job interview. Equally as bad, many never show the common courtesy of extending a sincere thank you to a networking contact who has gone out of his or her way to pave the way to an important networking contact or employer introduction. If I had to estimate, I would venture that fewer than 20 percent of job seekers ever take the time to extend this basic courtesy.

In this chapter, I will be discussing four types of thank you letters as follow:

1. Postinterview thank you letters to the hiring manager.
2. Postinterview thank you letters to interview team members.
3. Postinterview thank you letters to the staffing manager.
4. Networking thank you letters.

Following discussion of each of these type letters are some examples that you might use as models in crafting your own thank you letters.

Thank You Letters to Hiring Manager

If you send no other thank you letter following a job interview, you will want to send one to the hiring manager to whom you would be reporting should you be hired. This is especially true if you have a strong interest in the position for which you have applied.

When it comes to the job interview, I have witnessed several cases where a basic thank you letter sent to the hiring manager made the difference between who received the job offer and who didn't. A thank you letter not only shows that you were appreciative of the manager's time and effort, but, if well written, it is an excellent opportunity to again market your relevant skills and cite your interest and enthusiasm for the position. If interested in the job, why not take full advantage of this additional marketing opportunity.

Review of the following two thank you letter examples will show that this type of letter typically includes the following basic components:

SAMPLE A   *Hiring Manager Thank You Letter*

926 Dry Gulch Road
Hillsville, TX 21386
May 28, 2005

Ms Judith F. Ludwig
Director of Absorbent Research
Johnson Fiber Company
2665 Commercial Blvd.
Austin, TX 24385

Dear Judy:

I wanted to let you know how much I appreciated the opportunity to interview for the position of Senior Scientist in Absorbent Technology. I have been thinking about this opportunity most of the day. It seems like such a great fit for my qualifications and career interests!

With my Ph.D. in Material Science and expertise in fiber physics, I know I could make some real inroads in your desire to create super-absorbent materials for integration into your new disposable diaper product development program. I already have some creative ideas running around in my head that could help you meet the special challenge of greatly enhancing diaper absorbency and simultaneously reducing product weight.

I am looking forward to the next step in the employment process and hope to hear from you shortly.

Thank you again for your hospitality during my visit, and for a very interesting day!

Sincerely,

Barbara Carry

Barbara M. Carry

SAMPLE B   *Hiring Manager Thank You Letter*

503 Wellington Road
Grand Rapids, MI 13285
February 2, 2004

Mr. Raymond S. Langston
Director of Operations
Wolfson Manufacturing, Inc.
22 Johnson Road, South
Grand Rapids, MI 13448

Dear Ray:

Thank you for the opportunity to interview for the position of Procurement Manager at Wolfson Manufacturing. This is an exciting opportunity, and I look forward to the prospect of joining the company and working as part of your team.

Ray, I particularly enjoyed our extended discussion concerning the application of JIT principles as a viable vehicle for reducing raw material costs. As you know, I am a strong advocate of this approach. The JIT program I implemented at Dorsey Company, in fact, delivered more than $4 million annual cost savings to the company's bottom line.

As also discussed during our meeting, my training in TQM has also paid off. While at Dorsey, my use of TQM as the basis for establishing a rigid certification process for vendors resulted in a 35% drop in product rejection and reduction in production downtime of nearly 10%. This combination was credited with an additional $2.4 million annual cost savings. I sensed your interest in this approach and feel this is a fertile area for profit improvement at Wolfson as well.

Ray, I am very interested in the position at Wolfson, and would welcome the opportunity to become a valuable contributor to your operating team.

Thank you again for the opportunity to meet with you, and I look forward to hearing from you regarding next steps.

Sincerely,

George Zuckerman

George D. Zuckerman

1. Statement of appreciation for the interview.
2. Expression of interest in employment.
3. Reaffirmation of relevant qualifications.
4. Special value statement (optional).
5. Final thank you statement.

Remember, when writing this type letter, a little enthusiasm can go a long way! Managers invariably prefer candidates who show enthusiasm and strong interest in the position over others who don't. Such interest automatically suggests a higher motivation to perform the job. Most managers can't resist candidates who communicate their enthusiasm for the work.

Interview Team Thank You Letters

Although certainly not a requirement, it is a nice gesture to send a thank you letter to the members of the interview team who took time from their busy work day to spend time with you during your job interview. After all, you may find yourself a member of their work group, and a little courtesy can go a long way in setting the stage for a cordial working relationship.

Certainly, if interested in the position, taking a few minutes to express your appreciation can't hurt. Who knows, if you send your letter promptly, it may even arrive before they have a chance to send their interview evaluation form to the staffing manager. This could be just the thing that might tip the scales in your favor.

Where time allows, it is a good idea to personalize these letters as much as possible rather than send the same letter to all interviewers. This approach rings with a bit more sincerity than the one-size-fits-all approach and demonstrates your willingness to go the extra mile when it comes to personal relationships and the things that count.

Review of the following sample letters will show that both incorporate the same basic elements as follow:

1. Statement of appreciation for time spent with you.
2. Expression of interest in the position.
3. Reference to event that occurred or topic discussed during the interview discussion.

SAMPLE A   *Interview Team Thank You Letter*

102 Pine Ridge Trail
Boulder, CO 21859
September 22, 2004

Mr. William R. Decker
Senior Project Engineer
Fulton Paper Company, Inc.
Winslow, ME 23226

Dear Bill:

Thanks for spending the time with me during my recent interview at Fulton Paper. Your insights on the work environment at Fulton were particularly helpful and served to heighten my interest in working for the company. I am very interested in the Paper Machine Project Engineer position at Fulton and am looking forward to hearing from Don Mason concerning the outcome of my interview discussions.

I found our conversation about transpiration drying stimulating, and it served to enhance my appreciation for the state-of-the-art nature of Fulton's drying technology. This is a far cry from the old wire sections used in conventional papermaking, and I look forward to learning more about this exciting new approach.

Again, Bill, I appreciated the time you spent with me during our interview discussion, and would welcome the opportunity to work with you and the other members of the project engineering team should I have the opportunity to join your company.

Thanks again for your hospitality!

Sincerely,

Marian Flemming

Marian A. Flemming

SAMPLE B   *Interview Team Thank You Letter*

102 B Winding Lane
Cherry Hill, NJ 19227
October 20, 2006

Ms Sarah J. Bunting
Senior Sales Representative
HR Technologies, Inc.
2000 Cambridge Road
Westchester, NY 13228

Dear Sarah:

I enjoyed meeting you during my interview trip to HR Technologies and appreciated the time you spent helping me to understand sales opportunities at your company. I was impressed with the warmth and friendliness of the sales team, and I am very interested in working as a member of your group. You seem to enjoy working together.

Until you mentioned it, I hadn't realized that HR Technologies is now the market leader in the development and sale of competency-based human resources software, but after seeing the product, I can readily see why. I appreciated the software demonstration, and your patience and thoroughness in describing the product's functionality. This was particularly helpful!

I believe my prior experience, as an HR generalist, should prove a real asset in helping me quickly grasp the fundamental value of this product to the HR community. I look forward to the prospect of selling it to HR professionals, as I am convinced it will provide them with an excellent strategic tool that will enable them to make a substantive contribution to their companies.

Again, Sarah, I wish to thank you for your hospitality during my visit. I valued our conversation and would look forward to working with you as a fellow member of the sales team.

Sincerely,

John Barringsford

John T. Barringsford

4. Expression of appreciation for information shared with you.
5. Final thank you and reference to the possibility of working together.

Use of the sample letters as models for tailoring your own correspondence is bound to save you time and win a few points with prospective workmates.

Staffing Manager Thank You Letters

A brief thank you letter, addressed to the staffing or employment manager following a job interview, is a wise investment of your time. The fact that this individual has invested considerable personal time and effort in getting you to the interview stage is reason enough to send a thank you note. This does not even take into consideration the fact that this individual is often the person who will coordinate interview feedback from the members of the interview team and put together the offer recommendation as well as specifics of any job offer to be made. A little basic courtesy is in order if you are truly interested in the employment opportunity.

Although often discounted by the unknowing job seeker, the role of the staffing manager can sometimes be quite influential in the final employment decision. While working as an employment executive with the corporate employment function of a Fortune 100 company, I have personally witnessed numerous occasions when the persuasiveness of an employment manager was a major factor that either convinced a hiring manager to extend an employment offer or decline the employment candidate. So, don't just assume this individual is simply an administrative support person who has little or no impact on the employment decision. Such an assumption could prove fatal to your employment chances!

Elements of an effective staffing manager thank you letter typically include:

1. Appreciation statement for arranging the interview.
2. Statement of interest in the position.
3. Brief value statement—highlighting ability to make a contribution to the company.
4. Final thank you and statement of interest in receiving a job offer.

SAMPLE A *Staffing Manager Thank You Letter*

133 Winslow Road
West Chester, PA 19384
August 15, 2005

Ms Sandra Willingham
Manager of Corporate Staffing
The Baxter Corporation
18 Chemical Road
Plymouth Meeting, PA 19375

Dear Sandra:

I wanted to let you know how much I appreciated the opportunity to interview for the position of Research Scientist with Baxter, and your role in making this possible. This is an exciting opportunity, and I want to reaffirm my strong interest in this position!

The day was extremely informative, and I came away feeling stimulated by the dedication of your research staff and the professionalism of the work environment. This is certainly a team with whom I would enjoy working.

I feel that my M.S. from the Institute of Paper Chemistry, and more than 5 years of research experience in the development of new towel and tissue products, while at Stromberg Paper Company, should prove valuable assets to your company's product development efforts. I think I can make some valuable technical contributions in helping the product development group successfully address some of the adhesive challenges they are facing, since this is a specialty area where I have strong technical expertise.

Thank you again for an interesting and informative day. I am anxious to hear the results of our discussions and hope that the decision will be a positive one.

Sincerely,

John Thompson

John R. Thompson

SAMPLE B   *Staffing Manager Thank You Letter*

515 Lakeview Circle
Bellingham, WA 23177
May 4, 2005

Mr. Donald P. Jackson
Manager of Corporate Staffing
The Braxton Consulting Group
1200 Technology Place
Seattle, WA 23158

Dear Don:

I came away from Friday's interview at Braxton Consulting feeling very upbeat and with a high regard for your company's dedication and commitment to becoming the preeminent leader in the field of organization effectiveness consulting. Thank you for your role in making my visit possible.

I am genuinely excited about the prospects of joining your software development group as a key member of your product development team. I think my 15 years of HR generalist experience will prove quite beneficial in bringing improved clarity and focus to those areas of product functionality that will add greatest value in the eyes of the HR professional community. I already have some ideas in mind, which I feel will add considerable value to your exciting and revolutionary new software product.

It was certainly a pleasure to interview with Tim Jenkins and the other members of the research staff. I also found our discussion about the work environment and strategic vision of the company stimulating and thought provoking. Thank you for insight in these important areas.

Again Don, I thoroughly enjoyed my visit and look forward to hearing from you shortly. I am hopeful the decision will be a positive one, and that I will have the opportunity join your fine company.

Thank you.

Sincerely,

Bill Smith

William R. Smith

Close examination of the sample letters contained on the previous pages illustrates how these letter elements can be effectively incorporated.

Networking Thank You Letters

Too often persons go out of their way to help the job seeker without ever receiving a subsequent thank you letter expressing appreciation for their assistance or feedback from the job seeker on the results of their valuable advice and counsel. This is inexcusable!

As already noted in Chapter 10, it is believed that networking (i.e., personal help and valuable contacts of others) accounts for an estimated 70 percent or better of all job-hunting success. It seems incredible, then, that many job seekers fail to feed and nurture the very sources that are most likely to help them find that important next career opportunity. A simple thank you letter to those who help you with your job search seems a small price to pay.

Elements of an effective networking thank you letter typically include:

1. Statement of appreciation for assistance provided.
2. Feedback on the benefits realized from the contact's assistance.
3. Status of your job search.
4. Request for ongoing assistance.
5. Final thank you statement.

The following sample letters show how these elements can be used to produce an effective networking thank you letter.

SAMPLE A *Networking Thank You Letter*

106 Summit Avenue
Shillington, PA 19248
March 15, 2004

Ms Linda W. Langston
125 Flower Street
Wyomissing, PA 19274

Dear Linda:

Thank you so much for your advice and encouragement during our telephone conversation last Wednesday. It is comforting to know that when things seem a bit discouraging, there is a friend like you who is willing to lend a hand. I hope to have the opportunity to repay your kindness someday. Thank you for being there.

Linda, I wanted to let you know that your referral to Wayne Douglas at Carpenter Technology was particularly beneficial. Wayne has reviewed my resume, and I now have an interview set up for next Wednesday with the Engineering Manager. It seems they have an opening for a Metallurgical Engineer, and my background appears to be a good fit for their requirements. I am looking forward to this meeting and greatly appreciate your role in helping to make this possible.

I also appreciated your review of my resume and the several suggestions you made for improvement. I have incorporated many of your suggestions and feel, overall, that my resume is now a much more effective document. A second set of eyes is always helpful, especially where writing is concerned.

Although the first three weeks of my job search were a little discouraging, things are clearly beginning to get on track. Besides the opportunity with Carpenter, I have also had initial positive responses from both Reading Tube Corporation and the Dartmouth Metals Company. I suppose the anxiety associated with downsizing and layoff causes one to be a little impatient. I am confident now that things will work out just fine.

Again, Linda, thank you for your help and kindness. It was a real boost when I needed it most.

Please hang on to my resume and let me know of any other ideas or contacts that come to mind. I appreciate your continued support! Thanks for being such a good friend!

Regards,

Barbara

Barbara A. Swanson

SAMPLE B *Networking Thank You Letter*

203 Gator Way
Tampa, FL 13844
October 21, 2003

Mr. Wendell A. Pierson
Senior Financial Analyst
Capital Investments Corporation
300 Commerce Way
Jacksonville, FL 16338

Dear Wendell:

Thanks for meeting with me yesterday at Brickfords for our lunchtime discussion concerning my career search. It was a pleasure getting to know you, and I very much appreciated the time you spent and your sage advice. Thank you!

As you know, since 9/11 the financial community has been hit rather hard, and it is not the most ideal time to be thinking about a career move. Nonetheless, I am committed to making the transition and am determined that it will be a good one!

Wendell, I appreciated your review of my resume and comments for improvements. I have taken these to heart and incorporated them into this document. Overall, thanks to you, I feel my resume now has greater impact. Thanks for the suggestions!

This morning, at your recommendation, I spoke with both Peggy Jackson and Bob Taylor. Both have asked me for a copy of my resume, and will be passing it along to some of their contacts. Peggy was particularly encouraging and said she thought there may be an opportunity for someone with my credentials on their research staff. She is going to go to bat for me with Don Peterson, Foster Capital's Research Director. I will let you know the outcome.

Wendell, please hang on to my resume, and if you hear of anything, or can think of others in your professional network that might be good contacts, I would greatly appreciate hearing from you. I will make it a point to stay in touch and keep you advised of my progress.

Thank you, again, for your kindness and assistance!

Sincerely,

Warren

Warren D. Carter

INDEX